SPORTS

FACTS

WINDSURFER

ICE HOCKEY PLAYER

AMERICAN
FOOTBALL
PLAYER

DRAGSTER

P · O · C · K · E · T · S

SPORTS FACTS

Written by
NORMAN BARRETT

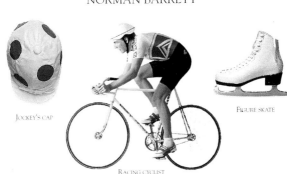

JOCKEY'S CAP

RACING CYCLIST

FIGURE SKATE

DK

A DK PUBLISHING BOOK

Project editor	Leo Vita-Finzi
Art editor	Jacqui Burton
Senior editor	Alastair Dougall
Senior art editor	Sarah Crouch
Picture research	Lorna Ainger
Production	Josie Alabaster
	Katie Holmes
US editor	Constance M. Robinson
US consultant	Don Wade

First American Edition, 1996
2 4 6 8 10 9 7 5 3 1
Published in the United States by
DK Publishing, Inc.,95 Madison Avenue
New York, New York 10016

Library of Congress Cataloging-in-Publication Data

ISBN 0-7894-1021-4

Color reproduction by Colourscan, Singapore
Printed and bound in Italy by L.E.G.O.

CONTENTS

HOW TO USE THIS BOOK

These pages show you how to use *Pockets: Sport Facts*.
The book is divided into nine parts. The first is
an introductory section. Those following contain
information on many sports. At the beginning of
each section there is a picture page with a list of
the sports covered by that section.

SPORTS FACTS
In this book, sports have been
divided into seven sections.
Within each section there is
detailed information on many
sports. At least one sport is
covered on every spread.

CORNER CODING
Corners of the main
section pages are
color-coded to
remind you which
section you are in.

☐ SPORT

☐ ATHLETIC SPORTS

☐ BALL SPORTS

☐ COMBAT AND TARGET
SPORTS

☐ WATER AND AIR SPORTS

☐ WINTER SPORTS

☐ SPORTS ON WHEELS

☐ ANIMALS IN SPORTS

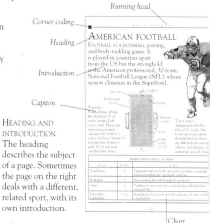

Running head

Corner coding

Heading

Introduction

Caption

AMERICAN FOOTBALL
FOOTBALL IS A RUNNING, passing,
and body-tackling game. It
is played in countries apart
from the US but the stronghold
is the American professional, 30-team,
National Football League (NFL), whose
season climaxes in the Superbowl.

Chart

AMERICAN FOOTBALL SCORING

HEADING AND
INTRODUCTION
The heading
describes the subject
of a page. Sometimes
the page on the right
deals with a different,
related sport, with its
own introduction.

CAPTIONS
Each illustration in the
book, whether photograph,
artwork, or diagram, is
accompanied by an
explanatory caption.

CHARTS
Charts appear on many
pages in the book. They
supply facts and figures.
The chart above shows
American football scoring.

RUNNING HEADS

The running heads act as a reminder of the section of the book you are in. The left-hand running head indicates the section and the right-hand one shows the subject of the page.

LABELS

For extra clarity, some pictures have labels. These identify a picture if it is not immediately obvious what it is from the text, or they may give extra information.

FEATURE BOXES

The feature boxes that appear on some pages contain detailed information and illustrations to explain a sport that is related to the main sport on the page.

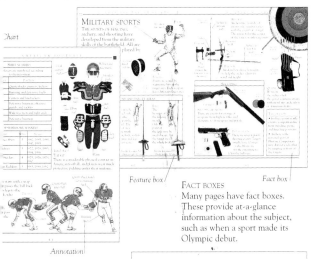

Chart

Feature box

Fact box

Annotation

FACT BOXES

Many pages have fact boxes. These provide at-a-glance information about the subject, such as when a sport made its Olympic debut.

ANNOTATIONS

Illustrations have annotations in *italics*. The annotation points out the features of diagrams and illustrations, often using leader lines.

INDEX

At the back of the book is an index listing every subject in the book. By referring to the index, information on particular topics can be found quickly.

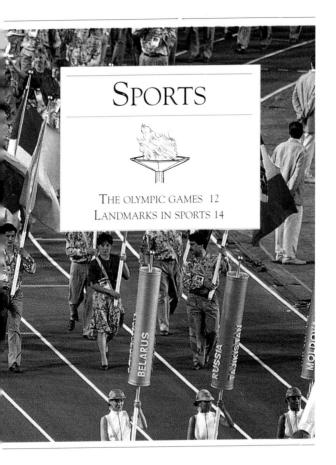

SPORTS

THE OLYMPIC GAMES

HELD EVERY FOUR YEARS, the modern Games began in 1896 as the brainchild of French scholar Pierre de Coubertin, who had been inspired by stories of the ancient Greek games. Separate Winter Olympics have been staged since 1924, and Paralympics for the disabled since 1960.

The interlocked rings represent the uniting of the five continents

OLYMPIC FLAME
The tradition comes from a practice of the ancient Greeks. Today, at the start of each Olympics, a torch is lit on Mount Olympus and carried by relay runners to the Olympic stadium.

COMPETITORS
Some 200 nations send more than 10,000 entrants to compete in nearly 30 sports. Most individual sports are limited to three or fewer entrants per country.

OLYMPIC RINGS
These rings adorn the Olympic flag

OLYMPIC GAMES VENUES					
YEAR	VENUE	YEAR	VENUE	YEAR	VENUE
1896	Athens, Greece	1932	Los Angeles, US	1972	Munich, Germany
1900	Paris, France	1936	Berlin, Germany	1976	Montreal, Canada
1904	St Louis, US	1948	London, UK	1980	Moscow, USSR
1908	London, UK	1952	Helsinki, Finland	1984	Los Angeles, US
1912	Stockholm, Sweden	1956	Melbourne, Australia	1988	Seoul, South Korea
1920	Antwerp, Belgium	1960	Rome, Italy	1992	Barcelona, Spain
1924	Paris, France	1964	Tokyo, Japan	1996	Atlanta, US
1928	Amsterdam, Holland	1968	Mexico City, Mexico	2000	Sydney, Australia

WINTER OLYMPIC GAMES VENUES

Year	Venue	Year	Venue	Year	Venue
1924	Chamonix, France	1960	Squaw Valley, US	1988	Calgary, Canada
1928	St Moritz, Switzerland	1964	Innsbrück, Austria	1992	Albertville, France
1932	Lake Placid, US	1968	Grenoble, France	1994	Lillehammer, Norway
1936	Garmisch, Germany	1972	Sapporo, Japan	1998	Nagano, Japan
1948	St Moritz, Switzerland	1976	Innsbrück, Austria	2002	Salt Lake City, US
1952	Oslo, Norway	1980	Lake Placid, US		
1956	Cortina, Italy	1984	Sarajevo, Yugoslavia		

REWARDS OF VICTORY
Professionals are now accepted in most major Olympic sports, but they are not paid for taking part. The only rewards are the gold, silver, and bronze medals won for coming first, second, or third.

WINNERS CELEBRATING, 1992

THE PARALYMPICS
Held just after the Olympic Games, usually at the same venue, the Paralympics include such sports as wheelchair racing, archery, tennis, and swimming.

1992
PARALYMPICS

OLYMPIC FACTS
• Despite boycotts and terrorism, the Olympics have been canceled only during war.

• 1,933 medals were won at the 1996 Games.

• The ancient Greek games were held for more than 1,000 years.

LANDMARKS IN SPORTS

The first sports, such as hunting and running, grew out of the need for survival. Others developed from religious rites. Today, huge numbers of people take part in sport for fitness and enjoyment, while others are professionals in a vast industry.

C.5000 BC		AD 129◦
c.5000 BC–c.776 BC	708 BC–c.AD 400	c.1100–1299

c.5000 BC–c.776 BC

- c.5000 BC Bowling game played in Egypt.
- c.3100 BC Polo played in India.
- c.2700 BC Wrestling and boxing practiced by early Mediterranean peoples.
- c.2000 BC Vaulting of bulls in Minoan festivals, Crete.

BULL VAULTING

- c.1550 BC Chariot racing in ancient Greece.
- c.1500 BC Archery practiced in ancient Greece.
- c.1350 BC A type of fencing with sticks developed in Egypt.
- 776 BC The first recorded Olympic Games held in Olympia, Greece.

708 BC–c.AD 400

- 708 BC Five-event pentathlon (discus, javelin, long jump, sprint, wrestling) introduced into the Olympics.
- 648 BC Horse racing makes its first Olympic appearance.
- AD 60–400 Building of the Colosseum in ancient Rome, where gladiators fight to the death. 200,000 fill the Circus Maximus for chariot racing.
- c.400 Religious ball game played by Maya Indians in what is now Mexico.

MAYAN BALL GAME

c.1100–1299

KNIGHTS AT A TOURNAMENT

- c.1100 Knights on horseback, in England and France take part in jousting tournaments to practice for warfare.
- 1174 Horse racing takes place in London, England.
- 1200 Pelota (a bowling game) is first played in France.
- 1200s Real tennis develops in France as a recreation in courtyards and monasteries.
- 1299 The first bowling green opens in Southampton, England.

1314–1740	1744–1829	1839–1847

• 1314 Mob football banned in London by edict of King Edward II.

• c.1410 Calcio, a type of

CALCIO: PUMPING UP THE BALL

football played 27-a-side and sponsored by the nobility, is played in Florence, reaching its height in the 1500s. (It is still part of an annual festival.)

• 1618 James I of England issues "The Book of Sports," a document to encourage the lawful pursuit of sports and counteract the negative influence of the Puritans.

• 1648 Jesuit missionary in Canada sees Huron Indian tribe playing "baggataway" and uses word "crosse" to describe their sticks: lacrosse is born.

• 1740 Oldest world championship founded – for real tennis.

• 1744 First known set of laws drawn up for cricket in London, England.

• 1777 The British explorer Captain Cook reports seeing surfers off the islands of Tahiti and Oahu. (In 1821, surfing was banned by missionaries who thought it was immoral.)

• 1811 The first outdoor gymnasium is opened by German schoolteacher Friedrich Jahn, founder of modern gymnastics and inventor of the parallel bars and rings.

FOOTBALL AT RUGBY SCHOOL

• 1823 Rugby is born when William Webb Ellis, a boy at Rugby school in England, picks up the ball and runs with it during a game of football.

• c.1829 Baseball, derived from the old game of rounders, is first played in the US.

• 1829 The first University Boat Race between Oxford and Cambridge takes place on the River Thames in London, England.

• 1839 By adding pedals to a scooterlike vehicle called the "draisienne," Scottish blacksmith Kirkpatrick MacMillan produces the first bicycle.

• 1839 The first Grand National Steeplechase is run at Aintree, England.

• 1843 First cross-country ski race organized at Tromsø, Norway.

• 1845 American sportsman Alexander Cartwright sets up the Knickerbocker Base Ball Club of New York, and writes the first set of baseball rules.

• 1846 Football rules drawn up in Cambridge, England, to co-ordinate the football codes.

TENPIN IN THE 1870s

• 1847 Tenpin bowling is born in Connecticut, when an extra pin is added to avoid a ban on the game of ninepins, which had been introduced from Europe.

1860

189

1860–1872	1872–1877	1879–1891

1860–1872

- 1860 The first British Open Golf Championship is held at Prestwick, Scotland.

- 1861 First modern hockey club, Blackheath, founded in London, England.

CYCLE RACE

- 1865 Boxing transformed from bare-knuckle prizefighting when Marquess of Queensberry draws up modern rules for gloved fighting.

- 1866 Australian rules football is first played, in Melbourne, Australia.

- 1866 First showjumping event, Paris, France.

- 1868 The first bicycle races are held in Paris.

- 1871 The Rugby Football Union is founded in England and consolidates the game in the UK and abroad.

- 1872 The first FA Cup competition takes place, the forerunner of other knock-out tournaments.

1872–1877

- 1872 Scotland win the first football international, beating England.

- 1873 Major Clopton Wingfield publishes a book of rules for "sphairistike" in England, and the game develops into lawn tennis.

- 1874 American football, half soccer and half rugby, develops when teams from Harvard and McGill University play the first match.

- 1875 Captain Matthew Webb is the first person to swim the English Channel.

EARLY ENGLAND TEST TEAM

- 1877 First cricket Test match, between England and Australia, at Melbourne, Australia.

- 1877 First Wimbledon lawn tennis championships.

- 1877 British Army officers draw up the first rules for badminton.

1879–1891

- 1879 The first ski jumping competition is staged near Oslo, Norway.

- 1880s A celluloid toy ball called Gossima from the US is brought to England and Ping-Pong, (table tennis) is born.

- 1882 Judo devised as a sport by Jigoro Kano in Japan.

- 1882 England-Australia cricket series now called "The Ashes."

- 1887 Young French scholar Pierre de Coubertin sows the seeds for the Modern Olympics in his campaign for a new approach to education.

- 1889 First speed-skating world championships are held in Amsterdam, Holland.

DE COUBERTIN

- 1891 Basketball invented in Massachusetts by Canadian sports instructor Dr. James Naismith.

1896

1995

1896–1924	1930–1968	1970–1995

1896–1924

•1896 First modern Olympics held in Athens, Greece, inspired by de Coubertin. Only men compete. Athletics events include the first marathon.

•1903 First Tour de France multistage cycle race.

EARLY AUTOMOBILE RACING

•1904 FIFA (Fédération Internationale de Football Association), soccer's world ruling body, founded in Paris, France.

•1912 Following experiments in Sweden, the modern pentathlon is included in the Stockholm Olympics.

•1922 The first slalom ski race takes place in Murren, Switzerland.

•1923 Speedway born in Australia.

•1924 First separate Winter Olympics. There are five sports: figure skating, ice hockey, Nordic skiing, bobsled, and speed skating.

1930–1968

•1930 Soccer's first World Cup held in Uruguay, contested by 13 teams and won by the host country.

•1930s Britain's Sir Malcolm Campbell breaks both the world land and water speed records.

•1936 Adolf Hitler uses the Olympics, held in Berlin, Germany, for Nazi propaganda purposes.

•1940s Black sportsmen win recognition in the US, including Joe Louis, world heavyweight boxing champion (1937–49), the first black professional American football players, and Jackie Robinson, the first black major league baseball player (1947).

•1950s Television becomes a major influence on the development of US sports.

CAMPBELL'S CAR, BLUEBIRD

•1960s Emergence of African athletes as a world force, particularly in running events.

•1968 Tennis becomes "open" (professionals may enter all competitions).

1970–1995

•1970 South Africa expelled from Olympic movement because of its government's apartheid policy.

•1970 Brazil becomes the only nation to win the soccer World Cup three times, so keep the trophy.

•1972 Terrorists kill 11 members of the Israeli team at the Munich Olympics.

•1978 Muhammed Ali regains the world heavyweight title for the third time: a record.

•1987 First rugby union World Cup.

•1980s–1990s Live international sports brought to worldwide television audiences by satellites.

RUGBY WORLD CUP, 1995

1980s–1990s Mass marathons (15,000 or more entrants) are staged around the world, some including wheelchair events.

1995 Rugby union, the last bastion of amateurism, allows players to become professionals.

ATHLETIC SPORTS

TRACK AND ROAD

MOST RUNNING EVENTS take place
on the track. They range from the
100 m to the 10,000 m. The most
famous road-running event is the
marathon, 26.21 miles (42.195 km)
in length. In major championships,
the marathon begins and ends in
the stadium, as do the walking races.

MARATHON
The race is named after
the battle of Marathon in
490 BC. A messenger ran
24 miles (39 km) to deliver
news of a Greek victory.

Synthetic surface, usually made of plastic or rubber

3,000 m, 5,000 m

Back straight

3,000 m steeplechase

RUNNING TRACK

200 m

1,500 m

110 m hurdles

Finishing straight

Finish line: the same for all events

Relays, 400 m, 400 m hurdles

100 m, 100 m hurdles

800 m

10,000 m

STAGGERED START
The 200 m, 400 m,
and 800 m races are
staggered. Longer
races start from
curved lines.

THE TRACK
Tracks used for
major competitions have
all-weather, synthetic
surfaces with eight lanes.
The starting lines for track
events are shown above.

Starting blocks provide the runner with a firm base from which to push off

LEVEL START
Only straight events, such as
the 100 m, have a level start.

HURDLE HEIGHTS

All hurdling events have 10 hurdles. They may be knocked over without penalty.

MEN'S	HEIGHT	WOMEN'S	HEIGHT
110 m	3 ft 6 in	100 m	2 ft 9 in
400 m	3 ft	400 m	2 ft 6 in

KENYAN STEEPLECHASER MOSES KIPTANUI

RELAY RACES

Relays in major championships are 4 x 100 m and 4 x 400 m. The baton must be exchanged within marked zones, and carried across the finish line.

PASSING THE BATON

The 4 x 100 m take-over zone measures 22 yd (20 m)

STEEPLECHASE

The 3,000 m steeplechase is run over 7.5 laps. On each lap there are three fixed hurdles; a water-jump lies inside the main track.

WALKING

Strict rules govern the walks: one part of a foot must always be in contact with the ground, and the leg must straighten momentarily as the foot touches the ground. The walks range from the 10 km to the 50 km.

Walker stretches out, completing the stride

Hips rotate to increase length of stride

Leg straightens as foot touches the ground

FIELD EVENTS

FIELD EVENTS TAKE PLACE in special areas inside the track. The jumping events consist of the long jump, triple jump, high jump, and pole vault. The throwing events comprise the shot, discus, hammer, and javelin. At the Olympic Games, women do not take part in the pole vault or hammer.

RAY EWRY

American Ray Ewry (1873-1937) won a record 10 Olympic gold medals in the early 1900s, all in the standing jumps (made without a run-up), which are no longer part of the official athletics program.

FOSBURY FLOP STYLE

Athlete twists onto her back as she jumps

HIGH JUMP
Competitors are allowed three jumps to make a clearance. As the bar is raised, they are eliminated until only the winner is left. The same applies in the pole vault

TRIPLE JUMP
This consists of a hop, step, and jump starting with a run-up to the take-off board and finishing in the sand landing-pit.

The athlete lands on the same foot used for take-off

HOP

THROWING EVENTS

THE SHOT
The athlete throws ("puts")
from the shoulder, and must
not step out of the circle.

THE JAVELIN
The throw is measured
to where the point first
touches the ground.

THE DISCUS
Usually thrown after a
couple of wind-up swings
and a full turn in the circle.

THE HAMMER
The hammer, a metal ball
on the end of a wire, is
hurled after 3 or 4 full turns.

LONG JUMP
This event calls for speed on
the runway before taking
off and landing
in the sand.

*Arms
stretched for
balance*

*Legs thrown
forward before
landing*

*Athlete throws arms
forward, ready
for landing*

STEP   JUMP

WORLD RECORDS

ON THE TRACK, world records are measured electronically to a hundredth of a second, field events to the nearest centimeter. Records must be ratified by the International Amateur Athletics Federation (founded in 1912). Here are records for major events through 1995.

FIELD EQUIPMENT

TRACK AND ROAD EVENTS (MEN)			
EVENT	DISTANCE	RECORD HOLDER	TIME
Sprints	100 m	L. Burrell (US)	9.85 secs
	200 m	P. Mennea (Italy)	19.72 secs
	400 m	B. Reynolds (US)	43.29 secs
Middle distance	800 m	S. Coe (UK)	1 min 41.73 secs
	1500 m	N. Morceli (Algeria)	3 mins 27.37 secs
	Mile	N. Morceli (Algeria)	3 mins 44.39 secs
Long distance	5,000 m	H. Gebresilasie (Ethiopia)	12 mins 44.39 secs
	10,000 m	H. Gebresilasie (Ethiopia)	26 mins 43.53 secs
Relays	4 x 100 m	US	37.40 secs
	4 x 400 m	US	2 mins 54.29 secs
Hurdles	110 m	C. Jackson (UK)	12.91 secs
	400 m	K. Young (US)	46.78 secs
Steeplechase	3,000 m	M. Kiptanui (Kenya)	8 mins 2.08 secs
Marathon	42.195 km	B. Dinsamo (Ethiopia)	2 hrs 6 mins 50 secs
Walks	20 km	B. Segura (Mexico)	1 hr 17 mins 25.6 secs
	50 km	R. Gonzalez (Mexico)	3 hrs 41 mins 38.4 secs

TRACK AND ROAD EVENTS (WOMEN)

EVENT	DISTANCE	RECORD HOLDER	TIME
Sprints	100 m	F. Griffith-Joyner (US)	10.49 secs
	200 m	F. Griffith-Joyner (US)	21.34 secs
	400 m	M. Koch (E. Germany)	47.60 secs
Middle distance	800 m	J. Kratochvilova (Czech)	1 min 53.28 secs
	1500 m	Qu Junxia (China)	3 mins 50.46 secs
	Mile	P. Ivan (Romania)	4 mins 15.61 secs
Long distance	3,000 m	Wang Junxia (China)	8 mins 6.11 secs
	5,000 m	F. Ribeiro (Portugal)	14 mins 36.45 secs
	10,000 m	Wang Junxia (China)	29 mins 31.78 secs
Relays	4 x 100 m	E. Germany	41.37 secs
	4 x 400 m	USSR	3 mins 15.17 secs
Hurdles	100 m	Y. Donkova (Bulgaria)	12.21 secs
	400 m	K. Batten (US)	52.74 secs
Marathon	42.195 km	I. Kristiansen (Norway)	2 hrs 21 mins 06 secs
Walk	10 km	N. Ryashkina (USSR)	41 mins 56.23 secs

FIELD EVENTS

EVENT	MEN'S RECORD HOLDER	RECORD	WOMEN'S RECORD HOLDER	RECORD
Javelin	J. Zelezny (Czech)	95.66 m	P. Felke (E. Germany)	80.00 m
Discus	J. Schult (E. Germany)	74.08 m	G. Reinsch (E. Germany)	76.80 m
Shot put	R. Barnes (US)	23.12 m	N. Lisovskaya (USSR)	22.63 m
Hammer	Y. Sedykh (USSR)	86.74 m	O. Kuzenkova (USSR)	68.15 m
High jump	J. Sotomayor (Cuba)	8 ft	S. Kostadinova (Bulgaria)	7 ft
Pole vault	S. Bubka (Ukraine)	20 ft	E. George (Australia)	14 ft
Long jump	M. Powell (US)	8.95 m	G. Chistyakova (USSR)	7.52 m
Triple jump	J. Edwards (UK)	18.29 m	I. Kravets (Ukraine)	15.50 m

STRENGTH AND STAMINA

THE MULTIEVENT sports are among the toughest of all, calling for speed and several skills, as well as strength and stamina. The decathlon (men) and heptathlon (women) combine track and field events. Weight lifting requires practiced technique and sheer strength.

AMERICAN HEPTATHLETE JACKIE JOYNER-KERSEE

COMBINED EVENTS
Competitors in the decathlon and heptathlon can claim to be the best all-around athletes. Sometimes they also specialize in one event as well.

TRIANGLE			
COURSE	SWIMMING	CYCLING	RUNNING
Short course	1.5 km	40 km	10 km
Long course	3.8 km	180 km	42.2 km

(Table title: TRIATHLON)

DECATHLON	
Points are awarded for each event according to standard tables of distances and times, and then added up.	
FIRST DAY	SECOND DAY
100 m race	110 m hurdles
Long jump	Discus
Shot put	Pole vault
High jump	Javelin
400 m race	1,500 m race

HEPTATHLON	
Points are awarded over seven events as in the decathlon. The heptathlon replaced the five-event contest for women (the pentathlon) in 1981.	
FIRST DAY	SECOND DAY
100 m hurdles	Long jump
High jump	Javelin
Shot put	800 m race
200 m race	

MODERN PENTATHLON
The five sports are usually held over four days, but in the 1996 Olympics, they were all staged on one day.
Fencing (Epée)
Swimming (freestyle: 300 m men; 200 m women)
Pistol shooting
Cross-country running (4 km men; 2 km women)
Riding (jumping course)

Events	Men	Women
Snatch	205 kg, Aleksandr Kurlovich (Belorussia)	115 kg, Li Yajuan (China)
Clean and jerk	253.5 kg, Andrey Chemerkin (Russia)	150 kg, Li Yajuan (China)
Overall	457.5 kg, Aleksandr Kurlovich (Belorussia)	265 kg, Li Yajuan (China)

SUPERHEAVYWEIGHT RECORDS – POST-1993 CATEGORIES

The lifter must stand completely still, with arms and legs fully stretched, for the lift to count

SNATCH
The lifter must raise the bar in a single movement until it is above the head with arms fully extended.

Unlimited time is allowed for recovery

Chalk is used to aid grip

CLEAN AND JERK
The bar is lifted to the shoulders ("clean") and may be rested before being raised above the head ("jerk").

Bar rested on collarbones

Bench height is adjustable

POWER LIFTING
This is another type of weight lifting. In the bench press, power lifters can raise more than five times their own body weight.

During the clean, the lifter must not let the elbows or upper arms touch the knees or thighs

ARTISTIC GYMNASTICS

IN MAJOR GYMNASTICS competitions, there are titles or medals for each individual event, plus overall and team titles. Judges award marks out of 10, depending on the difficulty of the routines and how well they are performed.

THE BEAM
This is probably the hardest of the women's events. The gymnast walks, runs, and leaps along a beam 4 in wide, and performs movements such as forward and backward somersaults in a routine lasting 70–90 seconds.

UNEVEN BARS
The gymnast moves rhythmically from one bar to another with smooth swinging and circular movements, constantly changing handholds and direction.

Safety mat

FLOOR EXERCISE
Women perform with music, men without. Tumbling, leaping, and balancing movements should use the full 39 ft 4 in-square matted area.

Gymnast ends the tumble ready for the next movement

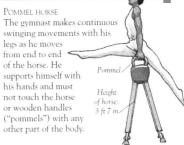

GYMNASTIC EVENTS

MEN	WOMEN
Horse vault	Horse vault
Floor	Floor
Parallel bars	Uneven bars
Horizontal bar	Beam
Rings	–
Pommel horse	–

POMMEL HORSE
The gymnast makes continuous swinging movements with his legs as he moves from end to end of the horse. He supports himself with his hands and must not touch the horse or wooden handles ("pommels") with any other part of the body.

Pommel

Height of horse: 3 ft 7 in

Some movements must be carried out slowly

HANDSTAND

Gymnast requires great strength

Width between bars: 16.5 in

PARALLEL BARS
This apparatus calls for a variety of skills: swinging movements mixed with balance positions. The gymnast sometimes lets go of both bars at the same time. Routines also include straddles and handstands. The wooden bars provide plenty of spring.

MOST WORLD AND OLYMPIC TITLES : MEN

GYMNAST	GOLD MEDALS	YEARS
Vitaly Scherbo (Belorussia)	15	1992-5
Boris Shakhlin (USSR)	10	1956-64
Leon Stukelj (Yugoslavia)	9	1922-8
Akinori Nakayama (Japan)	9	1966-72
Nikolay Andrianov (USSR)	9	1972-80
Dmitriy Bilozerchev (USSR)	9	1983-8
Joseph Martinez (France)	7	1903-9

MOST WORLD AND OLYMPIC TITLES: WOMEN

GYMNAST	GOLD MEDALS	YEARS
Larisa Latynina (USSR)	12	1956-64
Vera Caslavska (Czechoslovakia)	10	1962-8
Daniela Silivas (Romania)	9	1985-9
Lyudmila Tourischeva (USSR)	6	1968-76
Nadia Comaneci (Romania)	6	1976-80
Nelli Kim (USSR)	6	1976-80
Maxi Gnauck (E. Germany)	6	1979-83

RHYTHM AND ACROBATICS

RHYTHMIC GYMNASTICS, a sport for women, is performed to music with small hand apparatus. Sports acrobatics includes tumbling and balances similar to the repertoire of circus acrobats.

The ribbon must be circled and spiraled without touching any part of the body

RHYTHMIC GYMNASTICS
There are five individual events: rope, ribbon, clubs, hoop, and ball. Gymnasts use dance steps and graceful moves as they utilize their apparatus. There is also a group event, for teams of five.

Ball

Ribbon

Clubs

Rope

Hoops

A tumbling pass is performed on a straight, sprung track 82 ft long

The gymnast combines the use of the apparatus with body movements

EQUIPMENT
Each piece of equipment requires different techniques of the gymnast

Start of forward somersault

Legs open for one-footed landing

Moving into a round-off

TUMBLING SEQUENCE

SPORTS ACROBATICS

This branch of gymnastics derives from the circus. Balance work is performed in pairs (men, women, or mixed), trios (women) and fours (men) on a sprung floor 39 ft 4 in square. Tumbling, performed solo, consists of a series of somersaults, springs, and turns at high speed.

Free arm stretched out in line with body

Supported gymnast is the "top"

Gymnast on floor is the "base"

Partners use their weight against each other

A SIMPLE PAIRS BALANCE

Back somersault taken as high as possible

COUNTERBALANCE

Two-footed landing

Arms, legs, and back kept straight

Legs kept together and toes pointed during the back-flip

Legs brought down under body for landing

Finish must be upright and still

RHYTHM AND ACROBATICS FACTS

• Rhythmic gymnastics was introduced at the Los Angeles Olympics in 1984.

• Sports acrobatics is not an Olympic sport, but there are World Championships every year.

BALL SPORTS

ASSOCIATION FOOTBALL

ALSO KNOWN AS SOCCER or football, the
association game is the world's most
popular sport, widely played by women
as well as men, on every continent. A
match is played between two teams of ten
outfield players and a goalkeeper.

FOOTBALL
PLAYER

SOCCER FACT FILE

DURATION OF GAME
Two 45-minute halves
plus, in sudden-death
competitions, two
15-minute extra
periods, if needed.

MATCH OFFICIALS
The referee is
in sole charge,
assisted by two
linesmen on the
touchline with flags.

PUNISHMENT
The referee may
caution offending
players (yellow card) or
dismiss them (red card).

DRESS RULES
Shinguards, worn
under stockings,
are compulsory.

PLAYING THE GAME
The aim is to direct the ball into the
opponents' goal, normally using the
head or feet (hand or arm illegal).

Goals:
7.32 m wide;
2.44 m high

Goal
area

Length of
pitch:
90–120 m

Halfway
line

Center
circle

Touch
line

Penalty spot:
11 m from goal

Penalty area:
16.47 m deep;
40 m wide

EARLY 20TH
CENTURY SHOE

Width of pitch:
45–90 m

MODERN
SHOE

THE PITC[...]
Pitches vary in size so
penalty areas are alway[...]
the same. Goalkeepe[...]
may handle the ball with[...]
the penalty area unle[...]
one of their own tea[...]
has passed them the ba[...]

WORLD CUP FACTS
- Most World Cup wins: Brazil, four (1958, 1962, 1970, 1994).
- Highest score in World Cup: 10 - 1 (Hungary v. El Salvador, 1982).
- Most goals by a player in one game: Oleg Salenko, five (playing for Russia against Cameroon, 1994).

1994 WORLD CUP FINAL

THE WORLD CUP

Held every four years, the World Cup ranks with the Olympic Games as one of the world's great sports festivals. For the 1998 World Cup finals in France, qualifying competitions reduce 170 national teams to 32 finalists.

WORLD CUP TOP SCORERS

PLAYER	GOALS	YEARS
Gerd Müller (W. Germany)	14	1970–74
Just Fontaine (France)	13	1958
Pele (Brazil)	12	1958–70

WORLD CUP WINNERS

YEAR	VENUE	WINNING TEAM
1930	Uruguay	Uruguay
1934	Italy	Italy
1938	France	Italy
1950	Brazil	Uruguay
1954	Switzerland	West Germany
1958	Sweden	Brazil
1962	Chile	Brazil
1966	England	England
1970	Mexico	Brazil
1974	West Germany	West Germany
1978	Argentina	Argentina
1982	Spain	Italy
1986	Mexico	Argentina
1990	Italy	West Germany
1994	US	Brazil

WOMEN'S WORLD CUP

YEAR	VENUE	WINNING TEAM
1991	China	US
1995	Sweden	Norway

RUGBY UNION

PLAYED 15-A-SIDE, rugby union football features hand-to-hand passing, running, body tackling, and kicking. Once an amateur sport, it went "open" (allowing entry to professionals) in 1995, and its popularity is spreading.

PLAYING THE GAME
The eight forwards forage for the ball, feeding it to the half-backs who then dictate play. The other backs run, pass, and tackle.

PASSING

Fair throw

Forward pass

THROWING THE BALL
The ball may not be passed or thrown forward (in the direction of the opposition's goal line). The penalty is a scrum to the opposition.

Scrum half puts the ball in

Referee

THE SCRUM
A spectacular method of restarting play, scrums are formed by the two forward packs. The side putting in usually wins possession.

SCORING			
TYPE OF GOAL	POINTS	ACTION	
Try	5	Grounding ball on or over opponents' goal line.	
Dropped goal	3	Dropping ball and kicking it on half-volley over the crossbar.	
Penalty goal	3	Converting penalty kick.	
Conversion	2	Converting place-kick after try.	

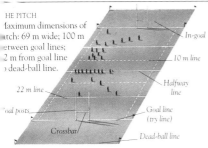

THE PITCH
Maximum dimensions of
pitch: 69 m wide; 100 m
between goal lines;
22 m from goal line
to dead-ball line.

22 m line

Goal posts

Crossbar

In-goal

10 m line

Halfway
line

Goal line
(try line)

Dead-ball line

RUGBY FACTS

• The women's World
Cup (now World
Championship) was first
played in Wales in 1991
and was won by the US.

• Seven-a-side
tournaments, such as
the Hong Kong Sevens,
are popular end-of-
season competitions.

RUGBY UNION WORLD CUP WINNERS

YEAR	VENUE	WINNING TEAM
1987	Australia and New Zealand	New Zealand
1991	British Isles and France	Australia
1987	South Africa	South Africa

RUGBY UNION WORLD CUP TOP-SCORERS

YEAR	PLAYER	MATCHES	POINTS
1987	Grant Fox (NZ)	6	126
1991	Roger Keyes (Ire)	4	68
1995	Thierry Lacroix (Fr)	6	116

SHIRT NUMBERS

Rugby players are numbered
according to their position.

SHIRT NUMBER	POSITION
1	Prop forward
2	Hooker
3	Prop forward
4	Lock forward
5	Lock forward
6	Flank forward
7	Flank forward
8	No.8
9	Scrum half
10	Fly half
11	Left wing
12	Center
13	Center
14	Right wing
15	Full back

Romania,
US, and
France,
(1924
entrants).

OLYMPIC RUGBY
Rugby has been an
Olympic sport four
times between 1900 and
1924, but never with more
than three entrants. The
World Cup is now rugby
union's premier competition.

RUGBY LEAGUE

FOR YEARS RUGBY LEAGUE was the professional offshoot
of the amateur union code. Teams of 13 play by
different rules to union. The game features passing and
running; possession must change after six tackles. The
sport has strongholds in Australia, Britain, and France

PLAY-THE-BALL

Acting half-back

Tackled player heels ball back

Marking player

A league scrum packs in a 3-2-1 formation

Scrum half

PLAY-THE-BALL RULE
A tackled player may
rise and drop the ball
before kicking it. He
normally heels it to a
teammate behind him.
After six consecutive
tackles, a team must
give up possession.

THE SCRUM
There are six forwards
in a league scrum, which
is used for restarts not
covered by kicks ("drop-
outs") or play-the-ball.

RUGBY LEAGUE SCORING		
TYPE OF GOAL	POINTS	ACTION
Try	4	Grounding ball on or over opponents' goal line.
Dropped goal	1	Dropping ball and kicking it on half-volley over the crossbar.
Penalty goal	2	Converting penalty kick.
Conversion	2	Converting place-kick after try.

Australian rules

This 18-a-side game is played mainly in Australia's Victoria State, where it has a fanatical following in and around the state capital, Melbourne. The Grand Final of the Australian Football League is the highlight of the season.

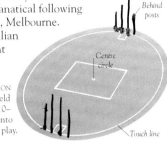

Width of goalposts: 6.4 m

Behind posts

Centre circle

Touch line

AUSTRALIAN RULES: FIELD AND DURATION
Rules is played on a huge oval field approximately 140–180 m long by 110–155 m wide. The game is divided into four quarters of 25 minutes actual play.

Chief umpire restarts game after a goal

STARTING PLAY

Ball thrown down in center circle

PLAYING THE GAME
Players kick, catch, and run with the oval ball. It must be bounced or touched on the ground every 10 m. The ball may not be thrown; players use the technique of holding the ball in one hand and palming or punching it, called "handballing."

SCORING

GOAL
Worth six points, a goal is scored by kicking the ball cleanly between the central posts.

BEHIND
Worth one point: kick between goal post and behind post or ball does not pass cleanly through goal posts.

AMERICAN FOOTBALL

FOOTBALL IS A RUNNING, passing, and body-tackling game. It is played in countries apart from the US but the stronghold is the American professional, 30-team, National Football League (NFL), whose season climaxes in the Superbowl.

End zone
Goalposts

Width of field: 160 ft

End line

THE FIELD
Painted lines divide the field into 5-yd strips, marked off every yard. The team in possession must advance the ball in a series of plays ("downs"), having four downs to gain 10 yd and start another first down.

Substitute benches

5 yd lines

Length of field: 120 yd

THE PLAYERS
American football is played 11-a-side, but teams may have more than 40 players: there are different elevens for offense and defense, and numerous special "teams."

AMERICAN FOOTBALL SCORING		
SCORE	POINTS	ACTION
Touchdown	6	Taking ball across opponents' goal line, or gaining possession within opponents' end zone.
Field goal	3	Place-kicking ball through the goal posts.
Safety	2	Tackling opponent who is carrying the ball behind his own goal line.
Point after touchdown	1 or 2	Goal kick (1) or pass into the end zone (2), after scoring a touchdown.

SHIRT NUMBERS

NFL players are numbered according to their position

SHIRT NUMBER	POSITION
1-19	Quarterbacks, punters, kickers
20-49	Running and defensive backs
50-59	Centers and linebackers
60-79	Defensive linemen, offensive guards, and tackles
80-89	Wide receivers and tight ends
90-99	Defensive linemen

TOP SUPERBOWL WINNERS

TEAM	WINS	YEARS
San Francisco 49ers	5	1982, 1985, 1989, 1990, 1995
Dallas Cowboys	5	1972, 1978, 1993, 1994, 1996
Pittsburgh Steelers	4	1975, 1976, 1979, 1980
Washington Redskins	3	1983, 1988, 1992

Oval leather ball

Helmet and face mask

Shoulder pads

Arm pads

Elbow pad

Rib pads

Leg pads

Cleated shoes

Pants

THE KIT
There is considerable physical contact in American football, and players wear much protective padding under their uniform.

THE SNAP
Each down starts with a snap. The center passes the ball back through his legs to the quarterback, who prepares to make the play, usually throwing a pass or slipping the ball to a running back.

Quarterback hands over to running back

Quarterback takes ball

THE SNAP

Center

Running back

CRICKET

WICKET

Bails

AN 11-A-SIDE GAME, the two teams alternate batting and bowling for one or two innings each. The bowling side must dismiss the batting side. First-class cricket is a two-innings game usually over three to five days, depending on the competition. Limited-overs cricket is a one-day, one-innings game.

BATTING
The batsman stands close to the crease and defends the wicket, trying to hit the ball and score runs. If he hits the ball in the air he risks being caught out by a fielder.

Sightscreen
Boundary
Outfield
Wicket
Pitch
Wicket
Outfield
Sightscreen

SCORING		
RUNS	ACTION	
1 or more	One run each time batsmen cross and reach opposite wicket.	
1	No ball: penalty for illegal delivery if no runs are otherwise made from it.	
1	Wide/bye/leg bye: runs scored without ball hitting bat, penalizing the bowling side.	
4	Ball reaches boundary after touching the ground.	
6	Ball reaches boundary without touching the ground.	

THE PITCH AND FIELD
Cricket is played on a pitch surrounded by a large field, often oval in shape. The pitch is a specially-prepared strip measuring 22 yd from wicket to wicket and 10 ft across. A line (the "crease") runs across the pitch 4 ft from the stumps.

BOWLING ACTION

Arm straight just prior to delivery

Foot not in front of crease

Crease

BOWLING
The bowling action is overarm. The arm must be straight in the act of delivery, and part of the front foot behind the crease. Bowlers take turns bowling "overs" of six (or eight) balls at alternate wickets.

TEST-PLAYING COUNTRIES

Test matches are internationals between major cricket-playing countries: the nine full members of the International Cricket Council. In Tests, normally played over five days, both sides have two innings.

TEAM	TESTS	WINS
Australia	551	227
England	712	244
India	292	53
New Zealand	236	33
Pakistan	223	61
South Africa	193	46
Sri Lanka	62	5
West Indies	314	123
Zimbabwe	13	1

CRICKET WORLD CUP WINNERS

The one-day game is the only manageable format for tournaments involving several nations. The World Cup carries great prestige.

YEAR	VENUE	WINNING TEAM
1975	England	West Indies
1979	England	West Indies
1983	England	India
1987	India/Pakistan	Australia
1992	Australia/New Zealand	Pakistan
1996	India/Pakistan/Sri Lanka	Sri Lanka

DISMISSING THE BATSMAN

BOWLED
The bowler's delivery hits the wicket. If the batsman obstructs with his body a ball that would have hit the wicket, he is "leg before wicket."

BOWLED

RUN OUT
The fielding side hit a wicket with the ball as the batsmen attempt a run.

RUN OUT

STUMPED
Batsman leaves the crease attempting to strike the ball early, and the fielding side hit the wicket.

STUMPED

BASEBALL

BASEBALL WAS DEVELOPED in
the US in the mid-1800s and
became the national sport.
North America is still the
stronghold of professional
baseball, but the game is
popular in many parts of
the world.

*Catcher rests
on one knee
between
pitches*

*He signals
what the next
pitch should be*

*Pitchers
throw the
ball at
more than
90 mph*

FIELDER'S
GLOVE

EQUIPMENT
Fielders wear gloves on
their nonthrowing hand
to catch the hard ball,
which has a cork center
wrapped by layers of yarn
encased in cowhide.

*Bats can be
up to 42 in
(107 cm)
in length*

BASEBALL
BAT

PLAYING THE GAME
The batter tries to hit the
ball, thrown ("pitched")
by the pitcher, and advance
around the bases without
being tagged or thrown out.
Each side has nine innings. An
inning ends when three batters are out.

Outfield

2nd base *Pitcher's
mound*

Diamond

3rd base *1st base*

*Foul
territory*

Infield

*Home
plate*

*Foul
territory*

THE FIELD
Fair territory consists of
an infield, whose points
are the three bases and the
home plate, and an outfield. Foul
territory lies outside these
areas. The pitcher throws from
a raised mound in the infield.

STRIKES AND BALLS

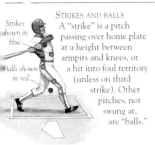

Strikes shown in blue

Balls shown in red

A "strike" is a pitch passing over home plate at a height between armpits and knees, or a hit into foul territory (unless on third strike). Other pitches, not swung at, are "balls."

PUTTING OUT THE BATTER

CAUGHT
Fielder catches the ball before it touches the ground ("on the fly").

STRIKE OUT
Three strikes are called against a batter.

CAUGHT

BUNT INTO FOUL TERRITORY
Batter attempts to tap the ball ("bunt") on the third strike, but the ball goes into foul territory.

BUNT

DOUBLE HIT

DOUBLE HIT
Batter deliberately hits the ball twice.

WORLD SERIES: MOST WINS

Each year, the top two teams in the US contest the World Series, a best-of-seven set of matches.

TEAM	WINS
New York Yankees	22
St Louis Cardinals	9
Philadelphia / Kansas City / Oakland Athletics	9
Brooklyn / Los Angeles Dodgers	6
Boston Red Sox	5
Pittsburgh Pirates	5
New York / San Francisco Giants	5
Cincinnati Reds	5

SOFTBALL

A scaled-down version of baseball, pitched underarm, softball is played over seven innings on a smaller diamond. The ball is larger and softer than a baseball. It is an Olympic sport for women.

KOREAN OLYMPIC PLAYER

STICK AND BALL GAMES

FIELD HOCKEY IS THE MOST widely played
team sport using a stick and ball. Others
include lacrosse, hurling, and shinty.
The aim of all of them is to propel a
ball into a goal using some form of stick.

Helmet v face-ma

EQUIPMENT

GOALKEEPER
Goalkeepers are well
protected from the hard
ball which can travel at
100 mph (160 km/h).

*Helmet has
a grille to
protect the
face*

GOALKEEPER'S
GLOVES

GOALKEEPER'S
HELMET

OUTDOOR
STICK

*The kicker enables
the keeper to use
his feet*

BALL

GOALKEEPER'S
KICKER

CLEATED
SHOE

INDOOR
STICK

Rubber cleats

FIELD HOCKEY
In this 11-a-side
sport, the players
use hooked sticks
to strike the small,
hard ball. They
may only use the
flat side of the stick.

GOALKEEP

OLYMPIC HOCKEY CHAMPIONS

India dominated men's Olympic hockey
from 1928 until they lost in the 1960 final
to Pakistan after a 30-game winning streak
during which they scored 196 goals to eight

TEAM (MEN)	WINS	YEARS
India	8	1928, 1932, 1936, 194 1952, 1956, 1964, 198
Pakistan	3	1960, 1968, 1984
Britain	3	1908, 1920, 1988
TEAM (WOMEN)	WINS	YEARS
Zimbabwe	1	1980
Netherlands	1	1984
Australia	1	1988
Spain	1	1992

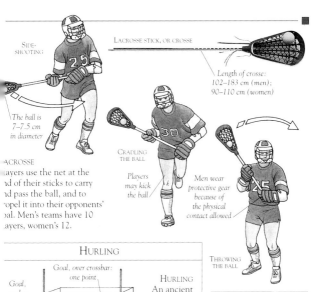

SIDE-SHOOTING

LACROSSE STICK, OR CROSSE

*Length of crosse:
102–183 cm (men);
90–110 cm (women)*

*The ball is
7–7.5 cm
in diameter*

CRADLING
THE BALL

*Players
may kick
the ball*

*Men wear
protective gear
because of
the physical
contact allowed*

THROWING
THE BALL

ACROSSE

layers use the net at the
nd of their sticks to carry
nd pass the ball, and to
ropel it into their opponents'
oal. Men's teams have 10
layers, women's 12.

HURLING

*Goal, over crossbar:
one point*

*Goal,
under
crossbar:
hree points*

HURLING
An ancient
Gaelic game
with teams of
15, hurling is
the national
sport of Ireland. Huge
crowds attend the annual
All-Ireland Championships.

Grip

*10 cm across
at widest*

*The hurley is
91 cm long*

HURLEY

STICK AND BALL FACTS

• Shinty is an ancient
Celtic game still played
in the Scottish
Highlands, with teams
of 12, using a curved
stick called a caman.

• Bandy, similar to
hockey, is an 11-a-side
game played on ice.
Now mainly popular
in the Baltic.

BASKETBALL

THIS FAST, END-TO-END GAME is popular in nearly 200 countries around the world. Teams of five play at any one time, and free substitution is allowed from teams of 10 or 12. The object is to throw or thrust the ball into the opposition's basket, using the hands.

End line

Free-throw line

THE COURT
The court has a hard surface, enabling players to bounce the ball as they run with it. Overhead lighting must not hinder players from shooting.

Field goals scored from within the semicircle: two points

Height of ring: 3.05 m

Field goals scored from outside the semicircle: three points

Games are often decided in the final seconds

STOP-WATCH

The court is 28 m long, and 15 m wide

BASKETBALL COURT

THE BASKET
At each end of the court is an iron ring with a cord net suspended from it that checks the ball as it passes through. The ring is attached to a backboard.

The ring is 45 cm in diameter

TIME RULES	
TIME LIMIT	ACTION
3 seconds	A player may remain in the restricted area between his opponents' end line and the free-throw line.
5 seconds	A player may hold the ball.
10 seconds	The team with the ball must move from the back court to the front court.
30 seconds	In some leagues, the team in possession must make a goal attempt.

OLYMPIC BASKETBALL CHAMPIONS

The Olympic basketball competition was first entered by men in 1936 and by women in 1976. Professional players were allowed to enter for the first time in 1992.

TEAM (MEN)	WINS	YEARS
US	10	1936, 1948, 1952, 1956, 1960, 1964, 1968, 1976, 1984, 1992
USSR	2	1972, 1988
Yugoslavia	1	1980

TEAM (WOMEN)	WINS	YEARS
USSR / CIS	3	1976, 1980, 1992
US	2	1984, 1988

US BASKETBALL PLAYER MICHAEL JORDAN

THE FOOTWEAR
Shoes have high ankle supports to take the strain of turning, jumping, and stopping.

BASKETBALL SHOE

DURATION OF THE GAME
There are two 20-minute or four 12-minute periods of playing time. Any player who commits five fouls (six in a 4x12-minute game) is expelled from the game.

NETBALL

PLAYING THE GAME
A seven-a-side game for women. The object is to throw the ball into the opposition's net. Players may not move with the ball but may pivot on one foot.

CHEST PASS

Players may hold the ball for 3 seconds

SHOULDER PASS

SHOOTING

BASKETBALL FACTS
• If a player is fouled in the act of shooting but still scores, the points count and a free-throw is awarded as well.

• The game was invented in 1891 in Massachusetts, by Canadian-born Dr. J. Naismith, who hung baskets from a balcony.

VOLLEYBALL

THE SIX PLAYERS on each team may use any part of their body above the waist to propel the ball over a high net into their opponents' court. A team has three touches to knock the ball back. Sets are up to 15 points; only the serving side can score.

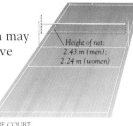

Height of net:
2.43 m (men);
2.24 m (women)

THE COURT
Service is from behind the end line. At service, players line up in two rows of three, but may move freely thereafter.

OVERHAND SERVE

UNDERHAND SERVE

PREPARING TO SPIKE (SMASH)

FOREARM PASS (DIG)

THE GAM
Forearms o
fingers are use
to knock the ba
up, ready for th
spike. The palm
are used to smas
the ball dow

CUBAN WOMEN'S TEAM WINNING THE 1992 OLYMPICS
THE GAME
A point is won if the ball lands in the opposition's court or they fail to return it.

TOP OLYMPIC VOLLEYBALL CHAMPIONS		
Volleyball has been included in the Olympic program for both men and women since 1964.		
TEAM (MEN)	WINS	YEARS
USSR	3	1964, 1968, 1980
US	2	1984, 1988
TEAM (WOMEN)	WINS	YEARS
USSR	4	1968, 1972, 1980, 1988
Japan	2	1964, 1976

BEACH
VOLLEYBALL
PLAYER

BEACH VOLLEYBALL
Played on sand two-a-side, on the same size court as the indoor game, beach volleyball appeared in the US in the 1940s. It spread to other countries in the 1960s and made its Olympic debut in 1996.

VOLLEYBALL FACTS

• The game was invented by American sports instructor William Morgan in 1895.

• Only in the deciding (fifth) set of a match may the side receiving serve score a point.

HANDBALL

THE GAME
Handball is a fast, seven-a-side sport, played on an indoor court with soccer-style goals. Players use their hands to dribble and pass the ball, and shoot from 6 m or more.

HANDBALL

Players must not hold the ball for longer than three seconds

Players may strike with any part of the body above the knees

LONG PASS   BOUNCING   SHOOTING   JUMP SHOT

TENNIS

THE OBJECT OF TENNIS is to hit the
ball over the net with a racket so
that it lands in the opposite court
and cannot be returned. Matches –
singles or doubles – are played in
sets: best of three, or best of five
in some men's tournaments.

*Using two
hands on the
racket restrict
reach but give
greater contro[l]*

THE COURT

Tennis is played on various
surfaces, both indoors and
outdoors. The doubles
court is larger than that
used for singles.

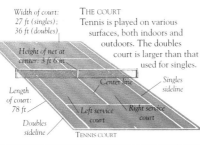

*Width of court:
27 ft (singles);
36 ft (doubles)*

*Height of net at
center: 3 ft 6 in*

Center line

*Singles
sideline*

*Length
of court:
78 ft*

*Left service
court*

*Right service
court*

*Doubles
sideline*

TENNIS COURT

PLAYING THE GAME
Strokes are normally made
with one hand holding
the racket. Many players
use two-handed shots for
more power and accuracy.

SERVICE ACTION

*Ball thrown
up high
enough so
that it can
be hit at
full stretch*

GRAND SLAM TOURNAMENTS		
To win the "grand slam" of tennis, a player must hold all four of the world's most coveted titles at the same time.		
TOURNAMENT	PLACE	SURFACE
Wimbledon	London, England	Grass
United States Open	Flushing Meadow, New York, US	Artificial material
Australian Open	Flinders Park, Melbourne, Australia	Synthetic grass
French Open	Stade Roland Garros, Paris, France	Clay

Top Grand Slam Winners (Singles)

Player (Male)	Total	Years
R. Emerson (Australia)	12	1961–67
B. Borg (Sweden)	11	1974–81
B. Tilden (US)	10	1920–30
Player (Female)	Total	Years
M. Court (Australia)	26	1960–73
H. Moody (US)	19	1923–38
M. Navratilova (US)	18	1978–90

MARTINA NAVRATILOVA

Scoring a Game

At deuce, play continues until one player gains a 2-point lead

Score	Points	Score	Points
Love	0	40	3
15	1	Deuce	3 (+)
30	2	Game	4 (+)

The Serve

The service is used to start each point in a game. Service alternates after each game. If the first serve to a point is a foul ("fault") then one more serve is permitted. If the second serve is a fault the point is lost.

Racket head launched at ball

Racket arm fully outstretched when hitting the ball

Racket arm bent back behind neck

In the follow-through, the racket arm comes across the body

Weight thrown forward

BADMINTON

PLAYED ON AN INDOOR court, the aim of the game is to hit the feathered shuttlecock (or "shuttle") over a high net into the opposition's court. The shuttle must be returned before it touches the ground.

Rigid wooden frame

19TH-CENTURY RACKET

Flexible frame

MODERN RACKET

Cork base SHUTTLECOCKS

Height of net: 1.55 m

Length of court: 13.4 m

Left service court

Right service court

BADMINTON COURT

THE COURT
A badminton court is similar to a tennis court, but with a higher net. Games are up to 15 points (11 in women's singles); matches are best of three games.

SERVING
Players serve underarm, and must strike the shuttle below waist level. A flick of the wrist may be used to change the placement of the serve at the last moment.

BADMINTON WORLD TEAM CHAMPIONS		
Both these competitions became biennial events in the 1980s. The men's competition is called the Thomas Cup; the women's, the Uber Cup.		
TEAM (MEN)	WINS	YEARS
Indonesia	9	1958, 1961, 1964, 1970, 1973, 1976, 1979, 1984, 1994
Malaysia	5	1949, 1952, 1955, 1967, 1992
China	4	1982, 1986, 1988, 1990
TEAM (WOMEN)	WINS	YEARS
Japan	5	1966, 1969, 1972, 1978, 1981
China	5	1984, 1986, 1988, 1990, 1992
US	3	1957, 1960, 1963
Indonesia	2	1975, 1994

Table tennis

Known in the late 19th century by the trade name "Ping-Pong," table tennis is now an international sport that earned Olympic status in 1988. It is played across a table, using a small paddle to hit a hollow plastic ball over a net. Games are played to 21 points; the winner must be two points clear.

THE SERVE
The ball must be thrown up from a flat hand (so no spin can be applied), and hit so as to bounce first on the server's side.

The blade must be flat and rigid

PADDLE SURFACE
The wooden blade may be covered with 2-mm pimpled rubber or 4-mm "sandwich" rubber.

Ball diameter: 38 mm

Length of table: 2.74 m

EARLY PING-PONG SET

Long-handled bats

THE TABLE
The wooden table is painted green with white lines. The line down the middle divides the court for doubles service.

Width: 1.525 m

TABLE TENNIS GRIPS

THE HANDSHAKE
Orthodox grip; forefinger lies along blade.

THE PENHOLDER
Asian grip: like holding a pen.

TABLE TENNIS FACTS

• Men and women play best of three or best of five games.

• The men's world team championship is called the Swaythling Cup; the women's, the Corbillon Cup.

SQUASH

A RACKET GAME played in an enclosed
court with four walls. Squash players
aim to hit the ball onto one or more walls
(it must hit the front wall) so that their
opponent cannot return it before it
bounces twice on the floor.

PAKISTANI
SQUASH PLAYER
JAHANGIR KHAN

*Reaching for a
high volley*

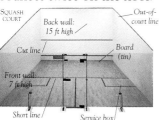

SQUASH
COURT

Back wall:
15 ft high

Out-of-
court line

Cut line

Board
(tin)

Front wall:
7 ft high

Short line

Service box

THE COURT
Red lines define where to stand when
serving and the areas within which
players may hit the ball.

PLAYING THE GAME
The ball must be
returned above the
board, which runs
across the bottom of
the front wall (1 ft
7 in high), before it
bounces on the floor.

SQUASH
RACKET

*Racket
frames may
be made of
graphite*

*Balls are 1.5 in
in diameter*

*Follow-
through to a
forehand lob*

SCORING
Games are played to
nine points, matches
to the best of three or five
games. Only the server can
win the point being
played, but loses serve
if the point is lost.

SQUASH BALL SPEEDS	
Balls are color-coded for speed. Faster balls are used by beginners.	
COLOR	SPEED
Yellow dot	Very slow
White dot	Slow
Red dot	Fast
Blue dot	Very fast

LONGEST-REIGNING WORLD OPEN CHAMPIONS

Both World Open Championships were first held in 1976; the Men's Open became an annual championship in 1979, the Women's in 1989.

PLAYER (MEN)	WINS	PERIOD
...nsher Khan (Pakistan)	7	1987–1995
PLAYER (WOMEN)	WINS	PERIOD
...usan Devoy (New Zealand)	5	1985–1992

SQUASH FACTS
• Jahangir Khan won the World Championship six times and the British Open a record 10 times.

• Luminous balls are used in televised events.

RACQUETBALL

Ball is pressurized for a fast game

...ACKET

EQUIPMENT
The rackets have large heads and short handles, with a loop for safety. A glove is usually worn on the racket hand.

GLOVE

Goggles protect the eyes

PLAYING THE GAME
Racquetball was invented in the US, where it is more popular than squash. World Championships have been held annually since 1982.

Shoes should provide a firm grip on the court

The court is 40 ft long and 20 ft wide and high

USE OF COURT
All walls and the ceiling are used except the top 8 ft of the back wall. As in squash, the ball must always hit the front wall and may bounce only once on the floor.

COMBAT AND TARGET SPORTS

MILITARY SPORTS

THE SPORTS OF FENCING, archery, and shooting have developed from the military skills of the battlefield. All are now Olympic sports, played by men and women.

FENCER

Wire mesh face mask

FENCING KIT
Protective clothing is worn. In competition, target areas are electronically wired to signal hits.

OVERJACKET

Woven metal thread records hits

Padding protects the sword hand

HEAD MASK

GAUNTLET

FENCING
Points are scored by registering hits on the target area. Each weapon has a different target area

WEAPONS AND TARGET AREAS

SABER
Hits may be scored with the whole of the front edge and the top third of the back edge of the saber. The target areas are the upper body and arms.

Weight: less than 500 g
Blade length: 88 cm

FOIL
Hits may be scored only with the point of the sword. The target area is the trunk of the body, so hits on arms and legs do not score.

Weight: less than 500 g
Blade length: 90 cm

EPEE
The heaviest of the fencing swords. Only the point of the épée may be used to score, but the target area is the whole body.

Weight: less than 770 g
Blade length: 90 cm

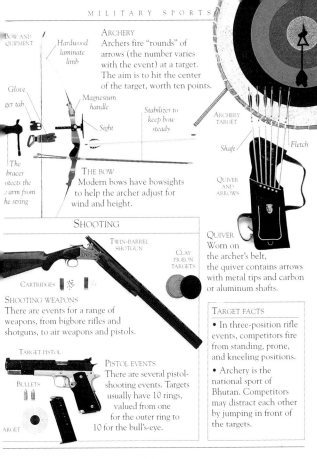

BOW AND
EQUIPMENT

Hardwood
laminate
limb

ARCHERY

Archers fire "rounds" of
arrows (the number varies
with the event) at a target.
The aim is to hit the center
of the target, worth ten points.

Glove

ger tab

Magnesium
handle

Stabilizer to
keep bow
steady

Sight

ARCHERY
TARGET

The
bracer
otects the
arm from
he string

THE BOW

Modern bows have bowsights
to help the archer adjust for
wind and height.

Shaft

Fletch

QUIVER
AND
ARROWS

SHOOTING

TWIN-BARREL
SHOTGUN

CLAY
PIGEON
TARGETS

CARTRIDGES

SHOOTING WEAPONS

There are events for a range of
weapons, from bigbore rifles and
shotguns, to air weapons and pistols.

QUIVER
Worn on
the archer's belt,
the quiver contains arrows
with metal tips and carbon
or aluminum shafts.

TARGET PISTOL

BULLETS

ARGET

PISTOL EVENTS

There are several pistol-
shooting events. Targets
usually have 10 rings,
valued from one
for the outer ring to
10 for the bull's-eye.

TARGET FACTS

• In three-position rifle
events, competitors fire
from standing, prone,
and kneeling positions.

• Archery is the
national sport of
Bhutan. Competitors
may distract each other
by jumping in front of
the targets.

BOXING

ONE OF THE WORLD'S oldest sports, boxing
is governed by strict rules that aim to
protect the boxers. But serious injuries,
even death, still occur occasionally, and
many would prefer to see the sport banned
for health reasons.

AMATEUR
BOXER

POINTS FOR PUNCHES
Boxers punch their
opponents on specific
areas. Fights are won on
points, a knock-out, or if
a boxer cannot continue.

FAIR PUNCH
Blows may be landed
on the front or side of
the head or trunk.

*Maximum size of
ring: 20 ft square*

FOUL PUNCH
A boxer may be
disqualified for hits
below the belt.

Red
corner

Blue
corner

GOOD PUNCHES
Punches are made
with the knuckle
part of the glove.

THE RING AND DURATION
A boxing ring is a padded
square surrounded by
ropes. At senior level,
an amateur bout is over
three 3-minute rounds
with intervals of one
minute. Professional bouts
last up to 12 rounds.

SELECTED BOXING WEIGHT CATEGORIES		
CATEGORIES	WEIGHT (PROFESSIONAL)	WEIGHT (AMATEUR)
Flyweight	108–112 lb	106–112 lb
Featherweight	122–126 lb	119–126 lb
Lightweight	130–135 lb	126–132 lb
Middleweight	154–160 lb	157–165 lb
Heavyweight	Over 190 lb	179–201 lb

XING KIT
ofessional boxers
ear shorts only.
mateurs wear
d or blue jerseys,
noting their corner.
heir gloves are the same
lor, with a white area for
nding scoring punches.

Lace-up
gloves
worn over
bandaged
hands

*Cutaway
shows
layers of
foam*

Soft
bandage

Gumshield

*Headguards
are worn in
amateur bouts*

*Lightweight
high-sided boots
support the ankles*

ose-
tting
orts

JOE LOUIS

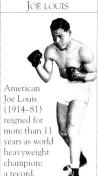

American
Joe Louis
(1914–81)
reigned for
more than 11
years as world
heavyweight
champion:
a record.

WRESTLING

Red
corner

Wrestling
surface

Blue
corner

*Wrestler's maximum
weight: 130 kg*

WRESTLING
Amateur wrestling has
two categories: freestyle
and Greco-Roman. Both
are Olympic sports.

WRESTLING CONTEST
The circle is 9 m in
diameter. Bouts last five
minutes or are won by
pinning the opponent's
shoulders to the mat.

*Some sumo wrestlers weigh
as much as four teenagers*

SUMO WRESTLING
In the ritualistic
Japanese sport of
sumo, contestants
try to push each
other out of a ring.
Most bouts last only
a few seconds.

MARTIAL ARTS

THE MARTIAL ARTS are combat skills that have developed in East Asia, often as a way of life or connected to religion. Only in the 1950s did their secrets become known in the West, and their popularity as sports o means of self-defense spread.

RED BELT
9TH–10TH DAN

BLACK BELT
1ST–5TH DAN

BROWN BELT
1ST KYU

BLUE BELT
2ND KYU

GREEN BELT
3RD KYU

ORANGE BELT
4TH KYU

YELLOW BELT
5TH KYU

JUDO BELTS
Belts range from
"kyu" (student)
to advanced
"dan" grades.

JUDO
Judo means "the gentle way." Players turn their opponent's strength and weight against them.

Contest area (approximately 9 m square)

Dange zone

JUDO HOLDS AND THROWS

SIDE 4-QUARTER HOLD

SINGLE WING

BODY DROP

ONE-ARM SHOULDER THROW

SHOULDER WHEEL

SWEEPING LOW THROW

STOMACH THROW

KNEE WHEEL

OTHER MARTIAL ARTS

KARATE
Strikes and kicks are used in karate, which means "empty hands."

AIKIDO
Meaning "the way of all harmony," aikido uses only defensive techniques.

JUJITSU
The ancient Japanese fighting art from which judo and aikido developed.

KENDO
Japanese sword-fighting, kendo is practiced in armor.

KARATE GLOVES
Gloves are used in some forms of karate for sparring or in certain competitions that allow contact to be made.

SEMICONTACT GLOVES

FOOT PROTECTORS,

These padded shoes slip over the feet

KENDO SWORD
The "shinai" is made from strips of bamboo tied together.

SHINAI

NUNCHAKU
This is a kung-fu weapon, originating in China. It is used in routines.

Wooden or rubber handle

Metal chain

Fingers hook over metal rings

FINGER GRIP
This is a device used to strengthen the fingers.

MARTIAL ARTS FACTS

• Judo became an Olympic sport for men in 1964 and for women in 1992.

• Taekwondo, a popular style of unarmed combat, means "kick-punch-way." It originated in Korea, and becomes a full Olympic sport at the 2000 Games.

BOWLING SPORTS

AIMING A BALL AT A TARGET has been a popular pastime for thousands of years. In bowls and boules, balls are rolled or thrown to get as close as possible to a target ball. In tenpin bowling, the aim is to knock over the target pins.

BOWLING IN FRANCE
Boules and the similar pétanque are French games played on rough ground, such as gravel. Metal balls are aimed at a smaller wooden target ball ("cochonet").

BOULES
The sets of boules have different markings so that the players can tell them apart. Each player uses two boules.

COCHONET

BOULE

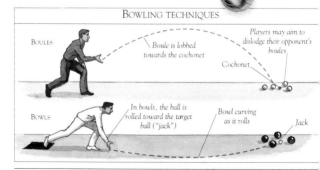

BOWLING TECHNIQUES

BOULES

Boule is lobbed towards the cochonet

Players may aim to dislodge their opponent's boules

Cochonet

BOWLS

In bowls, the ball is rolled toward the target ball ("jack")

Bowl curving as it rolls

Jack

BOWLS

The bowls (or "woods") are made of rubber or composite material. They are weighted ("biased") on one side to allow the player to curl them close to the jack.

Small ring: the bowl curves towards this side

Large ring: wood curves away from this side

TENPIN BOWLING

THE ALLEY

The pins are arranged in a triangle at the end of the alley.

BOWLING ALLEY

The lane is made of wood or plastic

The pins are set up automatically

The ball has three finger holes for grip

BOWLING BALL

Pins are made of wood coated with plastic

Brunswick
GRN2888
Black Beauty

PINS

STRIKE TACTICS

The aim is to knock down all ten pins. Players aim for the "pocket" between the lead pin and an adjacent one.

TENPIN BOWLING

A game consists of 10 frames, in each of which a player may have two attempts. Points are scored for each pin knocked down, with bonuses for getting 10 in one attempt (a "strike") or two attempts ("spare").

GOLF

THE GAME ORIGINATED in Scotland more than 500 years ago. The object is to knock a ball into a small hole using a club. There are normally 18 carefully constructed holes on a course. These must be played in succession using as few strokes as possible.

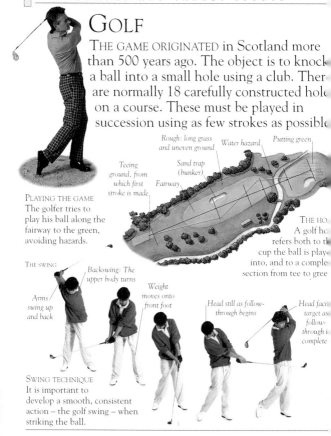

Rough: long grass and uneven ground

Water hazard

Putting green

Teeing ground, from which first stroke is made

Sand trap (bunker)

Fairway

PLAYING THE GAME
The golfer tries to play his ball along the fairway to the green, avoiding hazards.

THE HO...
A golf ho...
refers both to th...
cup the ball is play...
into, and to a comple...
section from tee to gree...

THE SWING

Backswing: The upper body turns

Arms swing up and back

Weight moves onto front foot

Head still as follow-through begins

Head facin... target as... follow-through i... complete

SWING TECHNIQUE
It is important to develop a smooth, consistent action – the golf swing – when striking the ball.

WOODS	IRONS	PUTTER
...d for the	Used for	Used on
...gest shots	a variety	the green
...a hole,	of shots	to roll the
...d often	between tee	ball to the
..."drive"	and green;	hole
...rst shot)	numbered	("putt")
	1–10	

EQUIPMENT

The clubs are carried in a golf bag or cart. Tees are used to support the ball for the first shot of each hole.

BALL ON TEE

GLOVE

A glove is worn on the front hand to aid grip

GOLF SHOES

...OLF CLUBS

...hoice of club depends on distance
...o be covered and the "lie" of the ball
...its situation on the ground). Players
...re allowed a maximum of 14 clubs.

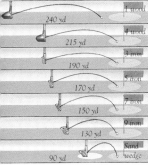

240 yd — 1 wood
215 yd — 4 wood
190 yd — 3 iron
170 yd — 5 iron
150 yd — 7 iron
130 yd — 9 iron
90 yd — Sand wedge

...ELECTED CLUB STRIKING DISTANCES

...TRIKING DISTANCES

...he diagram above compares the standard
...distance each club hits the ball. The
...ower-numbered woods or irons strike
...he ball farther, with a lower trajectory.

MAJOR GOLF TOURNAMENTS

There are four major professional golf tournaments. The team events are US v. Europe (men); US v. British Isles (women).

TOURNAMENT	FIRST HELD
British Open	1860
US Open	1895
US PGA	1916
US Masters	1934
Ryder Cup (men's team event)	1927
Solheim Cup (women's teams)	1990

RYDER CUP RESULTS

The Ryder Cup is a biannual competition between teams of 12, playing singles and in pairs (fourballs and foursomes), staged alternately in Europe and the US.

TEAM	WINS
US	23
Europe (formerly Great Britain and Ireland)	6

CUE AND BALL GAMES

SEVERAL GAMES ARE PLAYED on billiard or pool tables, using a stick called a cue to strike a white ball onto colored balls in order to "pot" them into the pockets. The most popular of these games are snooker and pool.

A wooden triangle is used to arrange the red balls

SNOOKER BALLS

REDS AND COLORS
Players first pot a red, then a chosen color, and so on until all reds are down. The colors are then potted in order of ascending value.

Length of table: 3.66 m

A corner pocket

A middle pocket

Cushion

Colors in position

Width of table: 1.86 m

SNOOKER TABLE

PLAYING THE GAME
Players score points for potting balls. They continue until they fail to pot a ball or play a foul shot, such as potting the wrong ball.

SNOOKER BALL VALUES		
These values also apply to penalties, except that the minimum penalty is four.		
COLOR	AMOUNT	POINTS
White	1	-
Red	15	1
Yellow	1	2
Green	1	3
Brown	1	4
Blue	1	5
Pink	1	6
Black	1	7

TOP WORLD SNOOKER CHAMPIONS		
PLAYER	WINS	PERIOD
Joe Davis (England)	15	1927–46
Fred Davis (England)	8	1948–66
Ray Reardon (Wales)	6	1970–78
Steve Davis (England)	6	1981–89
Stephen Hendry (Scotland)	5	1990–

TWO-PIECE CUE

*Screw
achment*

*Players chalk the tip of their
cue for added grip on the ball*

CHALK

STANDARD REST

SPIDER REST

EXTENDED
SPIDER REST

QUIPMENT
ues are made from wood,
th a leather tip. Rests
e used in positions
en the hand cannot
pport the cue.

SNOOKER FACTS

• Potting a black with all fifteen reds, and then all the colors, adds up to 147, the maximum "break" (score made in one turn at the table).

• When players cannot directly hit the required ball, they are said to be "snookered."

TOM REECE

In 1907, English billiards player Tom Reece made the highest-ever break – 499,135 – over several weeks of play. The rules have since been changed.

BILLIARDS
Players each have a white ball, one with two black spots. There is one red ball. Scores are made by potting the red, the other white, hitting both, or going in a pocket having hit another ball.

POOL

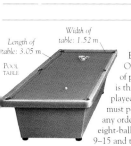

*Length of
table: 3.05 m*

*Width of
table: 1.52 m*

POOL
TABLE

EIGHT-BALL POOL
Of the many types of pool, eight-ball is the most widely played. One player must pot balls 1–7 (in any order) and then the eight-ball, the other player 9–15 and then the eight.

*Seven
colors*

*Seven
stripes*

THE BALLS
Numbers 1–7 are solid colors, while numbers 9–15 are striped.

WATER AND AIR SPORTS

YACHTING

ONE OF THE OLDEST FORMS of transportation, sailing
first became a sport in England in the 1600s.
Inshore racing takes place off the coast
around courses marked by buoys. Offshore
races cross seas or oceans. Yacht racing
became an Olympic sport in 1900.

TWO-PERSON DINGHY

Sail positioned to take advantage of the wind

Stern (back of boat)

YACHT RACING
Most racing is between boats
matched in type or class. In
this way skill, tactics, and
making best use of the
wind are all-important.

Bow (front of boat)

Hull made of reinforced plastic

YACHTING FACTS
• Some ocean races last
for days. Round-the-
world races take
months to complete.

• The yacht that won
the Olympic Flying
Dutchman title in
1968 was called
*Supercalifragilistic-
expialadocious*.

TACKING
A maneuver called tacking
is used to sail into the wind.
It involves sailing at an angle
to the wind, first one way,
then another, so that the
destination is reached.

Wind direction

Boat "goes about"

YACHT TYPES

OPTIMIST CLASS
A simple one-person dinghy designed as a training boat. It is also raced.

470 CLASS
A two-person dinghy, the 470 is an Olympic class for both men and women.

TORNADO
Another Olympic class, the Tornado is a two-person catamaran (twin-hull) boat.

FLYING DUTCHMAN
A two-person dinghy originating in Holland. Similar to the Olympic Laser class.

12-METER CLASS
The ocean-going 12-m is used in offshore races and is built to withstand heavy seas.

OLYMPIC CLASSES

There were eight yachting events in the 1996 Olympics, plus boardsailing (see page 76).

CLASS	TYPE	CREW (NUMBER)
Europe	Dinghy	Women (1)
Finn	Dinghy	Men (1)
Laser	Dinghy	Open (1)
470	Dinghy	Men/women (2)
Tornado	Catamaran	Open (2)
Star	Keelboat	Open (2)
Soling	Keelboat	Open (3)

AMERICA'S CUP
In 1851, the schooner *America* won a race that led to an event still held today.

AMERICA

SPINNAKER SAIL
Large, billowy sails called spinnakers are hoisted to make yachts sail faster in light winds.

SPINNAKER

WINDSURFING

THE SAILBOARD was developed from
an invention by a 12-year-old British
schoolboy in 1958. As a sport, windsurfing (also called boardsailing) was
pioneered in the US during the 1960s,
and now has worldwide popularity.

Sail

Mast, inside
the sleeve
of sail

Window

Boom

Universal joint
attaching mast
to board

Board

WINDSURFING BOARDS

Skeg

Daggerboard

DAGGERBOARD
This is a removable fin that stops the
craft from slipping sideways in the
water, like a boat's keel.

FUNBOARD
Funboards are
designed for sailing
in strong winds.
Spectacular jumps
can be made.

Flying leap out
of the waves

THE SAILBOAT
A simple, wind-propelled craft
with no rudder, it is steered
by means of the sail. The
sailor holds the boom, which
surrounds and supports the rig.

THE KIT
Life jackets and
wet suits may
be worn,
depending on
the conditions.

Helmet

Waist
harness

Short
wet suit
without
arms or
legs

Nonslip
shoes

COMPETITIONS
Racing takes place on
inshore courses marked by
buoys. Windsurfing became
an Olympic event in
1984. Other competitions
include freestyle, with
tricks and routines.

Surfing

A spectacular sport traditionally practiced on the beaches of Hawaii, Australia, and California, but now enjoyed wherever sea conditions are suitable. The sport became popular in the 1950s. The first world championships were held in 1964, and the first professional world championships in 1970.

Performing a move for the judges

COMPETITION SURFING
Surfers paddle out to sea on lightweight boards and "ride" the waves back to shore. They perform moves judged on style, grace, and timing. They also score points depending on the difficulty of the wave.

TOP PROFESSIONAL SURFING TOURNAMENTS

Each of these events on the professional surfing tour offers more than $100,000 in prize money.

EVENT	VENUE
Coke Surf Classic	Australia
Billabong Pro	Australia
Rip Curl Pro	Australia
Marui Pro	Japan
Quicksilver Pro	Indonesia
Rip Curl Pro Saint Leu	Reunion
CSI presents Billabong Pro	South Africa
US Open	US
Gotcha Lacanau Pro	France
Rip Curl Pro Hossegor	France
Quicksilver Surfmasters	France
Figueira Pro	Portugal
Rio Surf Pro	Brazil
Chlemsee Pipe Masters	US (Hawaii)

RIDING THE TUBE
The "tube" is the hollow formed under the crest of the wave. Skilled surfers can ride through this tube.

PERFECTING THE TURN
Turning looks easy when performed by experts, but timing is vital on moving waves.

SPEED ON THE WATER

BEING THE FASTEST at anything is a natural ambition in sports. Several people have lost their lives pursuing the world water speed record.

SPIRIT OF AUSTRALIA

SPIRIT OF AUSTRALIA
The water speed record was last broken in 1978 by Ken Warby in *Spirit of Australia*, a jet-engined hydroplane.

Hydroplanes have flat bottoms and skim across the water

A powerful engine thrusts the boat through the water

RACING POWERBOAT

Streamlined bow

POWERBOAT
Powerboat racing takes place inshore and offshore. Craft range from small boats with outboard motors to cabin-class powerboats

WATER SPEED RECORD PROGRESSION			
The official Water Speed Record is the average of a two-way run over a flying mile or kilometer. The records shown here stood at the start of each decade. The current record has stood since 1978.			
DATE	SPEED	BOAT	PILOT
1930	93 mph	*Miss America VII*	Gar Wood (US)
1940	142 mph	*Bluebird*	Malcolm Campbell (UK)
1960	260 mph	*Bluebird*	Donald Campbell (UK)
1970	282 mph	*Hustler*	Lee Taylor, Jr. (US)
1980	319 mph	*Spirit of Australia*	Ken Warby (Australia)

WATER SKIING

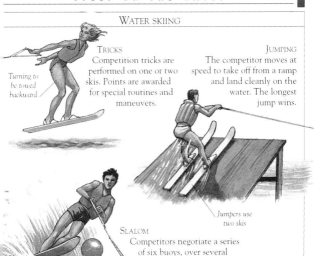

Turning to be towed backward

TRICKS
Competition tricks are performed on one or two skis. Points are awarded for special routines and maneuvers.

JUMPING
The competitor moves at speed to take off from a ramp and land cleanly on the water. The longest jump wins.

Jumpers use two skis

SLALOM
Competitors negotiate a series of six buoys, over several increasingly difficult runs.

T SKIING
t skiing is like owmobiling on water. eed and direction e controlled by ater jet.

WATER SKIING FACTS

• There are men's and women's competitions for the three water-skiing events, and an overall winner.

• A skier crossing from side to side in the wake of a boat can travel as much as three times as fast as the boat.

OARS AND PADDLES

THE SPORT OF ROWING, which includes sculling, dates back to the early 1700s in England. Both men and women now compete in Olympic events.

SCULLER

Rowers use one oar

Sliding seat

ROWER

Boats are made from wood or reinforced plastic

Scullers use two oars

SCULLING
Scullers use an oar in ea[ch] hand. There are singl[e], double, and quadru[ple] ("quad") scull eve[nts]

COXSWAIN ("COX")
Some boats have an extra person to steer: the cox. Crews of two and four may or may not have a cox. Eights are always coxed.

ROWING FACTS

• The standard course, on flat (nonflowing) water has six lanes marked, and measures 2 km for men, 1 km for women.

• The cox usually sits at the stern of the boat, but many pairs now seat the cox at the bow.

ROWING EVENTS	
EVENT	APPROXIMATE LENGTH OF BOAT
Single sculls	26 ft (8 m)
Double sculls	33 ft (10 ft)
Quadruple sculls	43 ft (13 m)
Coxless pairs	33 ft (10 m)
Coxed pairs (men only)	36 ft (11 m)
Coxless fours	43 ft (13 m)
Coxed fours (men only)	46 ft (14 m)
Eights	62 ft (19 m)

SCULLING TECHNIQUE

Single and double scullers use their sculls to steer. The quads use a foot-operated rudder.

The sculler leans forward, pulling the oars through the water

Sculler leans back, pulling the oars out of the water

The legs and then the back straighten

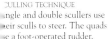

Blades held just above the water

ROWING TECHNIQUE

In the coxless events, one rower uses a foot-operated rudder (with wires) to steer.

The rowers lean forward, legs bent and arms straight

Rowers pull the blades through the water

Legs and then back straighten as stroke nears completion

Leaning back, arms bent, they pull the oars out of the water

CANOEING

KAYAK

The kayak has a closed deck. Canoeists sit inside, with legs outstretched under the deck.

Double-bladed paddle

CANADIAN CANOE

Most Canadian canoes have an open deck. The canoeist sits or kneels when paddling.

Single-bladed paddles

CANOEING

Canoe events include flat water racing, whitewater slalom, and wildwater.

Whitewater canoeists wear protective clothing

SWIMMING

SWIMMING DID NOT BECOME POPULAR until the 1800s for fear that it was a way of spreading disease. Swimming events in the first Olympic Games of 1896 took place in choppy seas. Held indoors since the 1948 Games, swimming is now a major Olympic sport, with 16 events for men and women.

SWIMWEAR
Goggles protect the eyes from chemicals in the water. A bathing cap covers the hair.

SWIMMER

Length of pool: 50 m

Starting block

SWIMMING POOL
Competitors dive from starting blocks and race in lanes. Timing is to 1/1000th of a second.

Lane width: 2.5 m

OLYMPIC SWIMMING EVENTS		
EVENT	MEN	WOMEN
Freestyle	50 m	50 m
	100 m	100 m
	200 m	200 m
	400 m	400 m
	1500 m	800 m
Backstroke	100 m	100 m
	200 m	200 m
Breaststroke	100 m	100 m
	200 m	200 m
Butterfly	100 m	100 m
	200 m	200 m
Individual medley	200 m	200 m
	400 m	400 m
Freestyle relays	4x100 m	4x100 m
	4x200 m	4x200 m
Medley relay	4x100 m	4x100 m

MEDLEY RACES: ORDER OF STROKES

The medley races incorporate all the swimming strokes:
the three regulated strokes and freestyle. In the relay, a
different swimmer takes each leg.

LEG	INDIVIDUAL MEDLEY	LEG	MEDLEY RELAY
1	Butterfly	1	Backstroke
2	Backstroke	2	Breaststroke
3	Breaststroke	3	Butterfly
4	Freestyle	4	Freestyle

SWIMMING FACTS

• In the heats of major
championships, the
swimmers with the best
times get the central
lanes in the next round.

• Short-course
swimming is held in
a 25 m pool.

SWIMMING STROKES

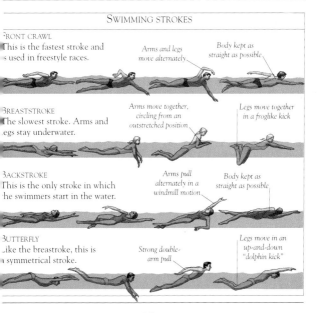

FRONT CRAWL
This is the fastest stroke and
is used in freestyle races.

Arms and legs move alternately

Body kept as straight as possible

BREASTSTROKE
The slowest stroke. Arms and
legs stay underwater.

Arms move together, circling from an outstretched position

Legs move together in a froglike kick

BACKSTROKE
This is the only stroke in which
the swimmers start in the water.

Arms pull alternately in a windmill motion

Body kept as straight as possible

BUTTERFLY
Like the breaststroke, this is
a symmetrical stroke.

Strong double-arm pull

Legs move in an up-and-down "dolphin kick"

SYNCHRO DUET

POOL SPORTS

THE OLYMPIC SPORTS of diving and synchronized swimming are similar to gymnastics in that judges award marks for style. There are two main diving events: springboard (3 m above the water) and highboard (10 m). Water polo is also an Olympic sport.

SYNCHRONIZED SWIMMING
In "synchro," as it is called, there are solo, duet, and group events, all for women. Swimmers perform gymnastic routines to music.

DIVING CATEGORIES

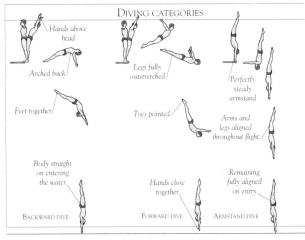

Hands above head

Arched back

Feet together

Body straight on entering the water

BACKWARD DIVE

Legs fully outstretched

Toes pointed

Hands close together

FORWARD DIVE

Perfectly steady armstand

Arms and legs aligned throughout flight

Remaining fully aligned on entry

ARMSTAND DIVE

OLYMPIC DEBUTS

Years when events were first staged in the Olympics.

EVENT	MEN	WOMEN
Highboard	1904	1912
Springboard	1908	1920
Water polo	1900	–
Synchronized swimming	–	1984

DIVING FACTS

• There are more than 80 standard dives.

• Maneuvers include somersaults, tucks, and pikes. Judges mark dives according to the degree of difficulty.

• Divers perform about 10 dives depending on the event, selecting from different diving categories.

WATER POLO
Played seven-a-side, water polo is like handball in the water. The object of the game is to throw the ball into the opposition's goal.

Pool: 30 m long;
20 m wide

DIVING CATEGORIES

Twisting in midair

Arms spread wide apart

Pike position

Hands touch toes

Pike position

Shoulders fall backwards for vertical entry

Body and legs straightened for flight and entry

Feet lift up for straight entry

TWIST DIVE   INWARD DIVE PIKED   REVERSE DIVE PIKED

AIR SPORTS

PEOPLE HAVE always longed to fly, and for hundreds of years have built many kinds of aircraft, including balloons, airplanes, and microlights. Most of these methods have developed into sports or pastimes.

SKYDIVING
Properly known as sport parachuting, skydiving includes landing on targets and joining up with other parachutists while free-falling.

HOT-AIR BALLOONING
Balloons are controlled by heating the air in the "envelope" to gain height and find a new wind direction.

Burner lit to inflate envelope with hot air

Top of balloon begins to rise

Pilot and passengers are carried in a wicker basket

AIR SPORTS FACTS

• Air racing takes place around a course (about 3 miles) marked by pylons.

• Hang gliders have reached heights of more than 2.5 miles.

• Jumping from several planes, skydivers may join in large formations.

MICROLIGHT

Engine

Fiberglass body

MICROLIGHT
Powered hang gliders, microlights can reach speeds of 100 mph. The pilot sits under the wings and steers by shifting body weight or by operating ailerons (flaps on the wings).

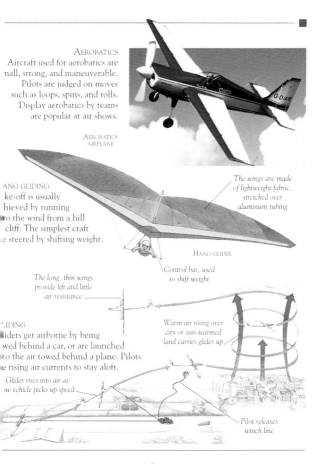

AEROBATICS

Aircraft used for aerobatics are small, strong, and maneuverable. Pilots are judged on moves such as loops, spins, and rolls. Display aerobatics by teams are popular at air shows.

AEROBATICS AIRPLANE

HANG GLIDING

Take-off is usually achieved by running into the wind from a hill or cliff. The simplest craft are steered by shifting weight.

The wings are made of lightweight fabric, stretched over aluminum tubing

HANG GLIDER

Control bar, used to shift weight

The long, thin wings provide lift and little air resistance

GLIDING

Gliders get airborne by being towed behind a car, or are launched into the air towed behind a plane. Pilots use rising air currents to stay aloft.

Warm air rising over city or sun-warmed land carries glider up

Glider rises into air as tow vehicle picks up speed

Pilot releases winch line

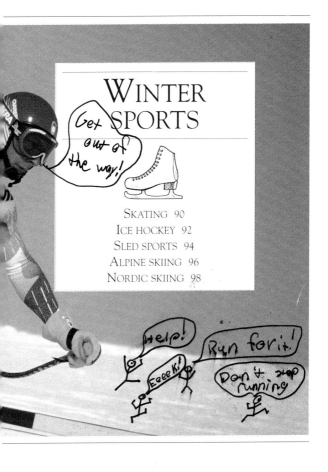

WINTER SPORTS

SKATING

FIGURE SKATING TAKES PLACE on an indoor ice rink. There are four events: men's and women's singles, pairs (mixed) and ice dancing. In speed skating, there is both long-track and short-track competition.

COMPETITION
Skaters perform set routines and free programs. Judges award marks for artistic impression and technical merit.

FIGURE SKATE
The skate's steel blade is 3 mm wide. Figure are skated on its edges.

Toe-rake helps in some jumps

Maximum width of rink: 30 m

RINK

Maximum length: 60 m

THE RINK
Figure skating usually takes place on an adapted ice hockey rink. To score well, skaters should cover the full area of th rink during the routine.

SKATING FACTS
• Norwegian figure skater Sonja Henie won 10 successive world titles (1927–36).

• American Eric Heiden won all five speed skating gold medals in the 1980 Winter games.

CAMEL SPIN

Preparation

Moving into the spin

One leg lifted behind and held parallel to the ice while spinning

SPINS
Spins should be performed on an axis around one spot with as little movement as possible from that spot.

JUMPS
[N]ames of jumps [su]ch as "axel," ["sa]lchow," and ["lo]op") depend on [ta]ke-off and landing.

LUTZ JUMP

One turn (two for double lutz) before landing

SPEED SKATING

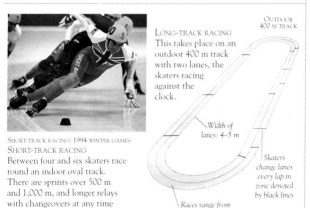

SHORT-TRACK RACING: 1994 WINTER GAMES

SHORT-TRACK RACING
Between four and six skaters race round an indoor oval track. There are sprints over 500 m and 1,000 m, and longer relays with changeovers at any time but the final two laps.

OUTDOOR 400 M TRACK

LONG-TRACK RACING
This takes place on an outdoor 400 m track with two lanes, the skaters racing against the clock.

Width of lanes: 4–5 m

Skaters change lanes every lap in zone denoted by black lines

Races range from 500 m to 10,000 m

ICE HOCKEY

PLAYERS SPEED OVER THE ICE at up to 50 km/h, making ice hockey fast and furious, with plenty of physical contact. It is played six-a-side; substitutes are allowed at any time. Teams continue short-handed when penalized players are serving time in the penalty box.

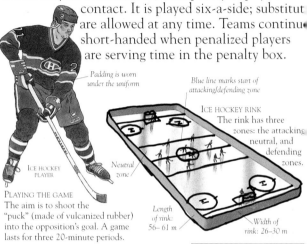

Padding is worn under the uniform

ICE HOCKEY PLAYER

Blue line marks start of attacking/defending zone

ICE HOCKEY RINK

The rink has three zones: the attacking, neutral, and defending zones.

Neutral zone

PLAYING THE GAME

The aim is to shoot the "puck" (made of vulcanized rubber) into the opposition's goal. A game lasts for three 20-minute periods.

Length of rink: 56–61 m

Width of rink: 26–30 m

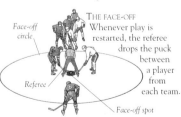

Face-off circle

THE FACE-OFF

Whenever play is restarted, the referee drops the puck between a player from each team.

Referee

Face-off spot

ICE HOCKEY PENALTIES	
Substitutes may come on for misconduct and match penalties.	
TYPE	MINUTES IN BOX
Minor	2
Major	5
Misconduct	10
Match	Rest of the game

locking pad

THE GOALKEEPER
Having the puck flying at them at 160 km/h, protection is needed by goalies.

Catch glove

Goalkeeper's pad

TOP ICE HOCKEY CHAMPIONS		
Ice hockey made its Olympic debut in the Summer games of 1920.		
TEAM	WINS	YEARS
USSR / Unified team	8	1956, 1964, 1968, 1972, 1976, 1984, 1988, 1992
Canada	6	1920, 1924, 1928, 1932, 1948, 1952
US	2	1960, 1980

THE EQUIPMENT

THE EQUIPMENT
Players wear ample protection against physical contact and the puck.

Helmet

Shoulder and chest padding

Elbow pad

Leg protector

Goalie's stick

Puck diameter: 7.62 cm

Skate

Glove

Player's stick

SLED SPORTS

HURTLING DOWN A STEEP, twisting track of packed ice at nearly 145 km/h is one of the most exhilarating – and dangerous – experiences in sport. Tobogganists and bobsled riders race to make the best time over the course.

RUNNING START TO A FOUR-MAN BOBSLED RUN

FOUR-MAN BOBSLED
The driver steers the bobsled with the help of two middle men, who shift their weight on the turns. The brakeman prevents skidding.

Brakeman

Fixed runners on back axle

BOBSLED RACING
The front runners of the sleds are turned with ropes or a steering wheel. Championship races are usually decided on the total time for four runs.

Sled made of steel and aluminum

Luge ridden face up, sitting or lying

LUGE TOBOGGANING
The luge is a one- or two-person toboggan with no brakes or steering. The riders, called "sliders," use their legs and shoulders to guide the vehicle.

OLYMPIC SLED EVENTS	
The toboggan has been held only at St Moritz Winter Olympics (1928 and 1948).	
EVENT	CREW
2-man bobsled	Men
4-man bobsled	Men
Single luge	Men/women
Double luge	Men
Toboggan	Men

ESTA RUN OF 1928

THE CRESTA RUN
Built more than 100
years ago at St. Moritz,
Switzerland. There is
a total drop of 157 m
over the 1,213 m
course. Competitors
reach speeds of nearly
145 km/h by the finish.

SLED FACTS
• Bobsleds were
invented by tourists in
Switzerland who lashed
two toboggans together
for more speed.
• American John
Heaton won both
Olympic silver medals
on the Cresta run – 20
years apart.

*Steel toe pieces,
called "rakes"*

*Helmet and
chin guard*

ELETON TOBOGGANING
here is no structure above
e runners – hence the term
keleton." The rider uses the toe
eces for braking, and steers by
fting his weight on the toboggan.

*Knee
pads*

DOGS AND SLEDS

SLED-DOG RACING
Popular in Canada, Alaska, the
northern US, and more recently in
Russia. A team has between
one and nine dogs,
usually Huskies,
Samoyeds, or
Malamutes. Racing
ranges from 40-km
"dashes" to 12-day
marathons.

*The "musher" guides his team
with cries of "Haw!" (turn left)
and "Gee!" (right)*

ALPINE SKIING

ALPINE SKIING INCLUDES slalom and downhill races, which are decided on time, and freestyle competitions which are judged on performance. Downhill racing dates back to 1911, slalom to 1922, and freestyle to 1966

Ski poles used for balance and to pick up speed

DOWNHILL SKIER

ALPINE SKI RACING

The skiers begin separately, starting an automatic timer. Slalom and giant slalom are decided on a two-run aggregate time, downhill on one run

Downhill course: 3–4.5 km (men); 1.5–2.5 km (women)

Super giant slalom: vertical drop: 500–600 m (men); 350–500 m (women)

Giant slalom vertical drop: 250–400 m (men); 250–350 m (women)

Slalom: 55–75 gates (men); 40–60 gates (women)

ALPINE EVENTS
The following are Olympic events for men and women, except ballet.
ALPINE SKI RACING
Slalom
Giant slalom
Super giant slalom
Alpine combined (downhill and slalom)
Downhill
FREESTYLE
Ballet
Moguls
Aerials

COURSES AND GATES

Flags marking the course are set on single poles for slalom gates, and double poles for the giant and super giant slalom races.

EQUIPMENT

SKIS AND POLES

The boot has a mechanism that releases it from the ski in a fall

SKI BOOT

Mittens are warmer than gloves

WHAT TO LOOK FOR
Most importantly, ski edges should be sharp and smooth. Bindings must not be loose or badly fitted.

DOWNHILL
The fastest race.
Skiers follow a set route, but have no gates to negotiate. Downhill skiers reach speeds of 140 km/h.

SLALOM
Alternate pairs of red and blue flags mark the course. Missing a gate means elimination. Top racers take gates at more than one a second.

FREESTYLE
Competitors perform on "moguls" (snow bumps), acrobatically off ramps in "aerials," and to music in ballet.

SPEED SKIING

TRAINING
To find the best position for skiing in special high speed events, some skiers practice on moving cars.

NORDIC SKIING

NORDIC SKIING COVERS two disciplines: cross-country ski racing and the spectacular ski jumping (in which only men compete). There are also relays and combined events (in which competitors both jump and race cross-country).

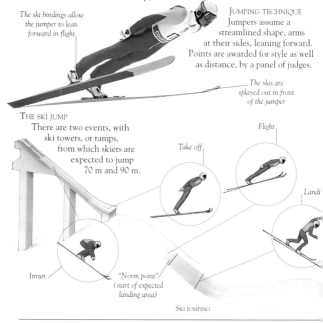

The ski bindings allow the jumper to lean forward in flight

JUMPING TECHNIQUE
Jumpers assume a streamlined shape, arms at their sides, leaning forward. Points are awarded for style as well as distance, by a panel of judges.

The skis are splayed out in front of the jumper

THE SKI JUMP
There are two events, with ski towers, or ramps, from which skiers are expected to jump 70 m and 90 m.

Flight

Take off

Landi

Inrun

"Norm point" (start of expected landing area)

SKI JUMPING

OLYMPIC EVENTS

The table below lists the Nordic skiing events, and who competes in them.

EVENT	COMPETITORS
km	Women
0 km	Men
Comb. pursuit	Men/women
5 km	Women
0 km	Men/women
x 5 km relay	Women
x 10 km relay	Men
Combined indiv.	Men
Combined team	Men
umping	Men

CROSS COUNTRY

There are two competition styles: freestyle (like a skater) and classical (a diagonal stride). Skiers, starting at intervals, are placed on time.

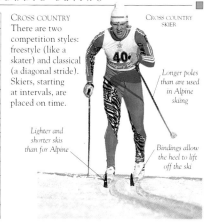

CROSS COUNTRY SKIER

Longer poles than are used in Alpine skiing

Lighter and shorter skis than for Alpine

Bindings allow the heel to lift off the ski

BIATHLON

BIATHLON

In a combination of cross-country skiing and rifle shooting, skiers carry their weapons on their backs and stop at intervals to shoot at targets.

The shooting stops are alternately from prone and standing position

Biathletes use small-bore rifles to fire five rounds at targets 50 m away

BIATHLON COMPETITIONS

Of military origin, biathlon competition was first held in 1912. It made its Olympic debut in 1960 for men, 1992 for women.

MEN'S EVENTS	WOMEN'S EVENTS
10 km	7.5 km
20 km	15 km
Relay 4 x 7.5 km	Relay 3 x 7.5 km

SPORTS ON WHEELS

FORMULA ONE

To most people, Formula One is the ultimate in motor sports: the best drivers in the world competing in high-speed grand prix races on the world's great circuits. Some 30 drivers contest the world championships over 17 races.

Smooth "slicks" for use in dry weather

Engine air intake

Body shell

WORLD CHAMPIONSHIP
Points go to the first six in each grand prix: 10-6-4-3-2-1. The driver with most points at the end of the season is World Champion.

Aerofoil

THE CARS
Formula One cars are light, single-seater, open-wheeled vehicles. The body – covered with the names of major sponsors – fits over a monocoque (one-piece) chassis.

THE 1995 MONACO GRAND PRIX
Checkered flag marks end of race

FLAG SIGNALS	
COLOR	MEANING
Yellow	Danger
Red and yellow stripes	Slippery track
White	Service car on track
Black	Car must stop in pits
Red	Race has been stopped
Green	All clear

TOP WORLD CHAMPIONS

DRIVER	WINS	YEARS
Fangio (Argentina)	5	1951, 1954–57
A. Prost (France)	4	1985–86, 1989, 1993
. Brabham (Australia)	3	1959–60, 1966
. Stewart (UK)	3	1969, 1971, 1973
J. Lauda (Austria)	3	1975, 1977, 1984
J. Piquet (Brazil)	3	1981, 1983, 1987
A. Senna (Brazil)	3	1988, 1990–91

F1 FACTS

• The record number of GP wins in a career is 44, by Frenchman Alain Prost, in 184 races.

• The Constructors' Championship, based on the placings of two cars, has been won most often by Ferrari (eight).

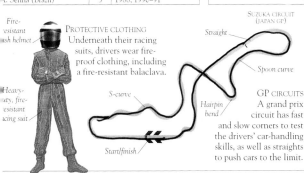

Fire-resistant ash helmet

PROTECTIVE CLOTHING
Underneath their racing suits, drivers wear fire-proof clothing, including a fire-resistant balaclava.

Heavy-uty, fire-resistant acing suit

SUZUKA CIRCUIT (JAPAN GP)

Straight

Spoon curve

S-curve

Hairpin bend

Start/finish

GP CIRCUITS
A grand prix circuit has fast and slow corners to test the drivers' car-handling skills, as well as straights to push cars to the limit.

FORMULA ONE ENGINE

THE ENGINE
Since 1989, when normally aspirated engines (without urbochargers to force fuel nto the cylinders to ncrease power) became he rule, V10 engines have ad most success.

RENAULT V10 ENGINE

Mounting point

Water outlet

Electronic control-unit connector

Exhaust pipe

RACING FORMULAS

FORMULAS EXIST IN RACING to ensure that similar machines are matched against each other. The drivers are not solely responsible for success. The whole team contributes – the manufacturer, the designers, and the mechanics all have vital roles to play.

Engine runs on methanol fuel

INDYC

INDYCAR
Indycar racin
takes place on ov
tracks and twisting roa
circuits, mostly in the U.

Heavier than a Formula One car

INDY 500
The most famous Indycar circuit is Indianapolis, which is 2.5 mi long. The Indy 500 race is held over 200 laps of the circuit.

Pit area

Start/finish

US STOCK CAR
These are hard-top vehicles based on regular road cars. They are modified to produce high speeds, but run on regular petrol.

STOCK CAR

STOCK CAR RACING AT DAYTONA, FLORIDA

STOCK CAR RACING
Chiefly run on the "super speedways" in the South. The ruling body is NASCAR (National Association for Stock Car Auto Racing).

OVAL RACING

Oval racing is a popular sport on small circuits of up to 400 m in Europe, but 800 m or more in the US. As racing tends to be organized locally, various types of cars and classes are involved.

Adjustable aerofoil

SUPER MODIFIED CLASS

Roll cage

OTHER FORMULAS

FORMULA 2 (F2)
A European F2 existed from 1967 to 1984 as a "nursery" for F1 drivers. It was revived in the UK in 1992.

Engine of up to 2,000 cc

F3 CAR

FORMULA 3 (F3)
The European F3 title is no longer contested, but these are still a popular formula in the UK.

F2 CAR

LE MANS

LE MANS 24-HOUR RACE
The world's most famous sports car race. Held since 1923 near Paris, France.

RACING FACTS

• In Indycar racing, the first 12 places earn points: 20-16-14-12-10-8-6-5-4-3-2-1.

• American Al Unser won the Indy 500 a record-equaling four times; his brother Bobby three times, and son Al Jr. twice.

OTHER MOTOR SPORTS

MOTOR SPORTS INCLUDE rallying and land speed record breaking as well as other types of racing. Karts are like racing cars in miniature. Dragsters race head-to-head over ¼-mile strips.

KART

Engine

Slicks used, as on racing cars

Throttle   Brake

KARTING
The simplest karts have a 100 cc engine and no gear box. The most powerful models can reach speeds of 149 mph.

DRAG RACING

Top-fueler, the fastest class of dragster

1 THE START
The race begins when the starting lights change from amber to green.

Engine behind driver

2 ACCELERATION
The lightweight, supercharged top-fuelers run on a type of rocket fuel.

Top-fuelers reach speeds of over 217 mph

3 THE FINISH
The most powerful of all racing cars may finish in under six seconds.

The winner goes through to the next round

4 BRAKING
A parachute is released at the back to help the dragster slow down.

LAND SPEED RECORD PROGRESSION

The official Land Speed Record is the average of a two-way run over a flying mile or kilometer. The records shown here stood at the start of each decade.

DECADE	SPEED	CAR	DRIVER
1900	65mph	Jenatzy (electric)	C. Jenatzy (France)
1910	126 mph	Benz	V. Héméry (France)
1920	150 mph	Packard	R. de Palma (US)
1930	231 mph	Irving-Napier	H.O.D. Segrave (UK)
1940	369 mph	Railton	J.R. Cobb (UK)
1950	394 mph	Railton	J.R. Cobb (UK)
1970	600 mph	Spirit of America Sonic 1	C. Breedlove (US)
1980	630 mph	Blue Flame	G. Gabelich (US)
1990	633 mph	Thrust 2	R. Noble (UK)

THRUST 2

Jet engine

THRUST 2
Richard Noble broke the land speed record in the specially built Thrust 2 on the flat, dry Black Rock Desert, Nevada.

RALLY DRIVING
Strengthened sedans compete over several days, losing points for exceeding set times.

RALLY FACTS

• The most famous rally is the Monte Carlo, first held in 1911.

• A navigator sits next to the driver and calls out detailed notes of the route, including every bend or change in surface of the course.

TOP RALLY CHAMPIONS

RIDER	WINS	YEARS
. Kankkunen (Finland)	4	1986, 1987, 1991, 1993
C.Sainz (Spain)	3	1990, 1992, 1995
W. Röhrl (W.Germany)	2	1980, 1982
M. Biasion (Italy)	2	1988, 1989

MOTORCYCLE RACING

MOTORCYCLE RACING TAKES PLACE on special circuits.
The world's leading manufacturers and drivers
compete in 12 or more grands prix each season for
world championships in several classes. Most races
are more than
100 km, which
is 20 or 30 laps
of the circuit.

Riders lean
over at steep
angles when
cornering

MOTORCYCLE
RACING

GRAND PRIX RACING
Points are awarded to the
first 10 in each grand prix:
15 points for first, one point for
tenth. The rider with the most
points in each class is the
champion of that class.

Light
aluminum frame

Streamlined
plastic body

Slicks (smooth
racing tires)

THE RACING BIKE
Racing motorbikes are powerful
machines designed for speed.
Classes range from 125 cc upward,
with a special class for sidecars.

MOTORCYCLE WORLD CHAMPIONSHIPS	
Changes in classes are shown since the first championships in 1949.	
CLASS	WORLD CHAMPIONSHIP
50 cc	1962–83
80 cc	1984–89
125 cc	1949–
250 cc	1949–
350 cc	1949–82
500 cc	1949–
750 cc	1977–79
Sidecar	1949–

SPEEDWAY TOP WORLD CHAMPIONS

Rider	Wins	Years
I. Mauger (New Zealand)	6	1968–70, 1972, 1977, 1979
O. Fundin (Sweden)	5	1956, 1960–61, 1963, 1967
B. Briggs (New Zealand)	4	1957–58, 1964, 1966
O. Olsen (Denmark)	3	1971, 1975, 1978
E. Gundersen (Denmark)	3	1984–85, 1988
H. Nielsen (Denmark)	3	1986–87, 1989

MOTORCYCLE FACTS

• Giacomo Agostini of Italy won the most motorcycle world titles ever: 15, between 1966 and 1975.

• There is a separate Superbike World Championship (750 cc).

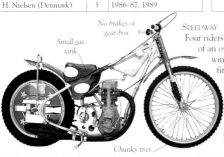

No brakes or gear-box

Small gas tank

Chunky tires

SPEEDWAY
Four riders race over four laps of an oval cinder track, winning points for the first three places. There are team matches and individual events in the speedway world championships.

SPEEDWAY BIKE

SIDECAR RACING

SIDECAR RACING
A racing sidecar is a motorbike and sidecar molded together into one unit. The driver and passenger work together as a team, the latter leaning over behind the driver to balance the bike when rounding a corner.

Taking a corner at speed

OFF-ROAD RACING

THE MOST POPULAR form of off-road motorcycle racing is motocross, which is the cross-country branch of the sport. Also called "scrambling," it takes place on special courses laid out in rough country.

OFF-ROAD
MOTORBIKE

MOTOCROSS WORLD CHAMPIONSHIPS	
Motocross stages about 12 grands prix in different countries, riders earning points towards a world championship.	
CLASS	WORLD CHAMPIONSHIPS
125 cc	1975–
250 cc	1962–
500 cc	1957–
Sidecar	1980–

MOTOCROSS
As many as 40 riders race over several laps of a winding, muddy, hilly course.

Well-padded seat

MOTOCROSS DES NATIONS – TOP COUNTRIES	
TEAM	WINS
Great Britain	16
US	13
Belgium	9
Sweden	7

Chunky-tread tires for gripping loose surfaces

MOTOCROSS BIKE
Bikes are light but strong, and are adapted to cope with rough, bumpy terrain, steep slopes, and changing surfaces.

Start of an international race

TRIALS RIDING

Trials is best known for six-day events, and includes slow sections over terrain such as loose rocks, water, mud, and steep climbs. Riders are penalized one point for putting a foot down, five for stopping.

ENDURO

ENDURO

Enduros are long-distance events similar to car rallies, testing both motorbike and rider over rough terrain. Riders, on modified motocross bikes, have set times to get from one checkpoint to the next. They do their own repairs.

STUNT RIDING

Display teams on bikes perform tricks, routines, and stunts, such as riding through fire and jumping over buses.

Riding through a ring of fire

OFF-ROAD FACTS

• Belgian Joël Robert has won a record six world championships, all in the 250 cc class (1964, 1968–72).

• Spaniard Jordi Tarres won a record four trials championships (1987, 1989–91).

CYCLE SPORTS

CYCLE RACES RANGE from sprints held over 1,000 m t
multistage road races lasting several weeks. The chie
track events are sprinting
and pursuit. There are also
points races – awarded at
intervals to the first three
crossing the line.

Helmet is
compulsory

Strong,
lightweight
frame

ROAD-RACING
BIKE

ROAD RACING
Road races take place over
single stages or several stages,
with aggregate time deciding
finishing position. In road time
trials, riders set off at intervals.

TYPICAL TOUR
ROUTE

TOUR DE FRANCE
The world's top
road race, held
over three weeks.
Team-mates help
their top rider.

*The Tour often enters
nearby countries*

Polka dot: rider
with most points
from climbing
stages

Yellow:
race leader

Green: rider
with most points
from sprints

TOP TOUR DE FRANCE WINNERS		
RIDER	WINS	YEARS
J. Anquetil (France)	5	1957–64
E. Merckx (Belguim)	5	1969–74
B. Hinault (France)	5	1978–85
M. Indurain (Spain)	5	1991–95

COLOR CODES
The leading riders in the Tour de Franc
may be identified by the color of their
shirts. The yellow jersey is worn by the
current race leader on aggregate time.

PURSUIT RACING

Riders start on opposite sides of the track. The race is decided on time or if one rider catches the other. Men ride 4,000 m, women 3,000 m.

No gears or brakes

PURSUIT BICYCLE

Ultra-lightweight with short wheelbase

Deeply curved drop bars

SPRINT BICYCLE

SPRINTING

Riders spend much of the race jockeying for position on the banked track, before making a dash for the line on the last lap.

OLYMPIC TRACK EVENTS	
There was men's cycling in the first modern Games (1896), but no women's until 1984.	
EVENT	COMPETITORS
Sprint	Men/women
Time trial	Men
Pursuit	Men/women
Team pursuit	Men
Points race	Men/women

MOUNTAIN BIKE RACING

Typical decline on mountain course

THE NEW OLYMPIC DISCIPLINE

A young but rapidly spreading sport, mountain biking gained Olympic status in 1996.

Gear shifters easy to reach while standing up

Chunky tires

Steel alloy frame

MOUNTAIN BIKE

THE BIKE

Mountain bikes are built to survive rough handling over rocky terrain.

Relaxed crouch position

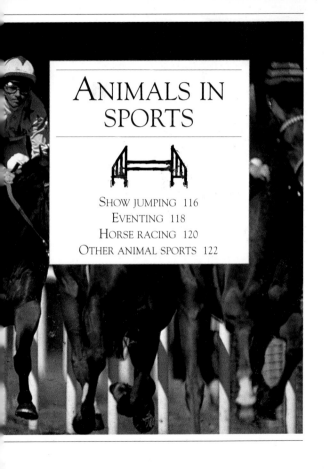

ANIMALS IN SPORTS

SHOW JUMPING

MEN AND WOMEN COMPETE with each other on the same terms in equestrian events, of which show jumping is the most popular. Riders take their horses around a course of varied obstacles (jumps).

TAKING A FENCE

A horse may clip a fence; faults are incurred only if part of it is dislodged

COMPETITION
There may be more than one round in a competition. A rider incurs "faults" for any errors. Those with the fewest faults jump off against the clock.

KIT AND TACK

RIDING HAT

Chin cup keeps hat in place

Pelham, a type of bit

BITS

SADDLE

Boots with no buckles or laces to catch in the stirrup

KIT
Riders must wear a hard hat or crash helmet and formal dress for competition.

Bridle, made of adjustable lengths of leather

GIRTHS

116

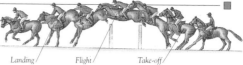

JUMPING TECHNIQUE
The rider bends forward from the hips and, on landing, straightens body.

Landing   Flight   Take-off

SHOW JUMPING COURSE

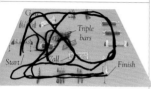

Gate / Triple bars / Start / Wall / Finish

OBSTACLES
Obstacles must be jumped in a set order between start and finish.

SHOW JUMPING FAULTS

ERROR	FAULTS
Fence (or part of fence) down	4
Foot in water	4
Refusal	3
2nd refusal	6
3rd refusal	Elimination
Fall (horse or rider)	8
Exceeding time allowance	1/4 per second
Taking jumps out of sequence	Elimination

FENCES

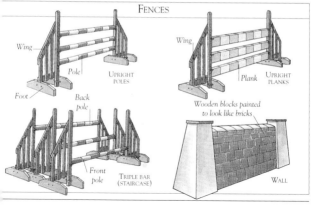

Wing
Pole
Foot
UPRIGHT POLES

Wing
Plank
UPRIGHT PLANKS

Back pole
Front pole
TRIPLE BAR (STAIRCASE)

Wooden blocks painted to look like bricks
WALL

EVENTING

In a three-day event, riders take their horses through three disciplines over three days. Dressage is a test of the rider's skill and the horse's obedience. Speed and endurance is the major event with four phases; it is worth the most points. The final event is show jumping.

CLEARING A JUMP ON THE CROSS-COUNTRY PHASE

CROSS-COUNTRY PHASE

Part of speed and endurance, it includes all kinds of obstacles, from water and slippery grass banks to solid walls and drops.

CROSS-COUNTRY
The cross-country is a tough phase of the event and riders can easily be injured in a fall.

The helmet may be covered with colorful silk

Body protector worn under colored top

EVENTING FACTS

• All three equestrian disciplines have been regular Olympic events since 1912. There are individual and team competitions.

• Outside the Olympics and world championships, the major international competition is at Badminton, in the UK.

SPEED AND ENDURANCE EVENT

Penalty points are incurred for exceeding the time allowances on all phases, for falling, or refusing any obstacles in the steeplechase and cross-country phases.

PHASE	DISTANCE	DETAILS
A. Roads and tracks	16–20 km	Trot or slow canter
B. Steeplechase	Approx. 3.5–4 km	9 or 10 fences
C. Roads and tracks	16–20 km	Trot or slow canter
D. Cross-country	Up to 8 km	28–32 obstacles

TOP HAT

CLEARING A FENCE

SHOW JUMPING
In eventing, the jumps in the show-jumping stage are not very high. But they test a horse's fitness after the speed and endurance event of the second day.

[DR]ESSAGE OUTFIT
[Fo]r competition, riders [wea]r a formal tail coat [an]d a top hat. Military [dr]ess is also acceptable.

THREE BASIC DRESSAGE PACES

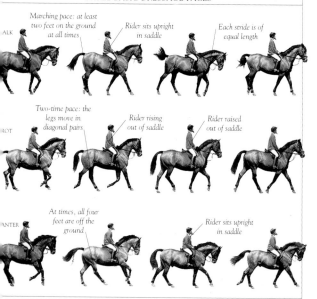

[W]ALK — Marching pace: at least two feet on the ground at all times

Rider sits upright in saddle

Each stride is of equal length

[T]ROT — Two-time pace: the legs move in diagonal pairs

Rider rising out of saddle

Rider raised out of saddle

[C]ANTER — At times, all four feet are off the ground

Rider sits upright in saddle

HORSE RACING

HORSE RACING DATES back to ancient times. The Thoroughbred horses used in racing are all descended from three original Arab stallions. The sport is now divided into flat racing and jumping (hurdles and steeplechase).

HORSE AND RIDER

Flat race jockeys are light – some may ride at 44.5 kg or less

Pocket for lead weights used to handicap horses with the best race records

THE KIT

JOCKEYS' KIT
Jockeys wear a crash helmet under their cap and carry a whip, the use of which is regulated.

Shirts (silks) and cap in owner's colors

Helmet covered in silk

THE THOROUGHBRED
Racehorses must be Thoroughbreds. They were first bred in Europe in the late 17th century.

FLAT RACING
Flat races are for horses of two years and over. Most races are between five furlongs and 1.5 miles.

JUMPING

Hurdle races, from 2 to 3.5 miles long, are for 3-year-olds and over. Steeplechases, over 2 to 4.5 miles, with fences, ditches and water jumps, are for 4-year-olds and over.

STEEPLECHASE

PALIO

PALIO
The Palio is a horse race that takes place every summer in the main square of Siena, Italy. The race has been run since medieval times.

MAJOR HORSE RACES

The first five are the English "Classics" for 3-year-olds, as are the Irish and Kentucky Derbys. The Melbourne Cup and the Grand National are handicaps. (f = furlong)

RACE	COURSE	DISTANCE	TYPE
2,000 Guineas	Newmarket, England	1 mile	Flat
1,000 Guineas (fillies)	Newmarket, England	1 mile	Flat
Derby	Epsom, England	1 mile, 4 f	Flat
Oaks (fillies)	Epsom, England	1 mile, 4 f	Flat
St Leger	Doncaster, England	1 mile, 6 f 132 yd	Flat
Irish Derby	The Curragh, Ireland	1 mile, 4 f	Flat
Arc de Triomphe	Longchamp, France	2,400 m	Flat
Kentucky Derby	Churchill Downs, US	1 mile, 2 f	Flat
Melbourne Cup	Melbourne, Australia	3,200 m	Flat
Grand National	Aintree, England	4 miles, 4f	Steeplechase
Cheltenham Gold Cup	Cheltenham, England	3 miles, 2 f	Steeplechase
Champion Hurdle	Cheltenham, England	2 miles	Hurdle

OTHER ANIMAL SPORTS

ANY ANIMAL THAT CAN be ridden can be raced, from elephants to ostriches. Some, such as dogs and pigeons, can be trained to race by themselves. Horses have always been the favorite sporting companion; rodeo, trotting, and polo horses all have strong followings.

The sulky is a light cart with bicycle-type wheels

Trotting horses are called standardbreds

TROTTING
A form of harness racing, the horses run with a "diagonal" gait (the two hooves touching the ground at any time are diagonally opposite). The driver sits in a "sulky."

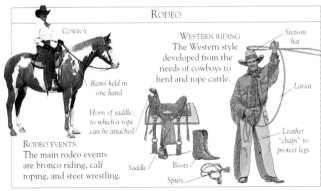

RODEO

COWBOY

WESTERN RIDING
The Western style developed from the needs of cowboys to herd and rope cattle.

Stetson hat

Lariat

Reins held in one hand

Horn of saddle, to which a rope can be attached

Leather "chaps" to protect legs

RODEO EVENTS
The main rodeo events are bronco riding, calf roping, and steer wrestling.

Saddle

Boots

Spurs

POLO

Gloves

Helmet

Long brown boots

Knee-pads

Mallet

PLAYING THE GAME
Played four-a-side. Riders use long mallets to strike a small white ball into the opposition's goal. It was last an Olympic sport in 1936.

Fast, nimble ponies

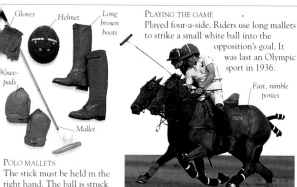

POLO MALLETS
The stick must be held in the right hand. The ball is struck with the side of the mallet.

The dogs wear colors according to their number

GREYHOUNDS RACING ROUND A CORNER

GREYHOUND RACING
Specially bred greyhounds chase an electric rabbit round a track over distances between 230 yd and 1,203 yd. Races may involve six or eight dogs.

ANIMAL SPORTS FACTS
• Specially bred homing pigeons are raced over as far as 621 miles. Released from the same place, they are "clocked on" when they return.

• Pato is an Argentinian horseback game. Riders throw a six-handled leather ball into a goal. It resembles a cross between polo and basketball.

Index

Acknowledgements

Dorling Kindersley would like to thank: Hilary Bird for the index; Caroline Potts for picture library services; Norman Barrett for use of his picture library.

Photographers:
Peter Chadwick; John Garrett; Philip Gatward; Dave King; Kevin Mallet; Ray Moller; Tim Ridley; Dave Rudkin; Karl Shone; Chris Stevens; Matthew Ward; Jerry Young.

Illustrators:
Clive Spong; Sebastian Quigley (Linden Artists); Peter Bull; Nick Hewetson; Richard Hook; Bob Langrish; Angus McBride; Alex Pang; Rodney Shackell; Rob Shone; John Temerton; Eric Thomas; Richard Ward; Gerald Wood; John Woodcock.

Picture credits: t = top b = bottom
c = center l = left r = right
The publisher would like to thank the following for their kind permission to reproduce the photographs:

Action Plus/ Peter Tarry 67br; Allsport/ Markus Boesch 51tl, Simon Bruty 119tr, Mike Cooper 21tr, Gray Mortimore 45br; Norman Barrett 15tl, c, br, 16tl, c, br, 17tl, 22cl, 66tl, 71cl, 75br, 79bl, 95tl, 104br, 105tr, 111bl; Colorsport 10-11, 13cr, 18-19, 35tl, 53tr, 58-59, 118tl, 121tl/ Andrew Cowie 26tr, 84tl, SIPA/ P. Curtet 111tl; The Image Bank/ Per Eriksson 95br; LAT Photographic 102cl; Sporting Pictures (UK) Ltd. 13bl, 17cr, 32-33, 49tr, 50bl, 77tr, 88-89, 91cl, 94tl, 98c, 99tr, 100-1, 109br, 114-5, 123tr, b; Tony Stone Images 111cr.

Every effort has been made to trace the copyright holders and we apologize in advance for any unintentional omissions. We would be pleased to insert the appropriate acknowledgement in any subsequent edition of this publication.